Dark
Matters

A Manifesto for the Nocturnal City

Dark Matters

A Manifesto for the Nocturnal City

Nick Dunn

Winchester, UK
Washington, USA

First published by Zero Books, 2016
Zero Books is an imprint of John Hunt Publishing Ltd., Laurel House, Station Approach,
Alresford, Hants, SO24 9JH, UK
office1@jhpbooks.net
www.johnhuntpublishing.com
www.zero-books.net

For distributor details and how to order please visit the 'Ordering' section on our website.

ISBN: 978 1 78279 748 7
978 1 78279 747 0 (ebook)
Library of Congress Control Number: 2016939766

A CIP catalogue record for this book is available from the British Library.

Design: Stuart Davies

Printed and bound by CPI Group (UK) Ltd, Croydon, CR0 4YY, UK

We operate a distinctive and ethical publishing philosophy in all
areas of our business, from our global network of authors to
production and worldwide distribution.

CONTENTS

For Sarah

Nick Dunn is the author of numerous books on architecture, art practices, design processes and urbanism. He is Chair of Urban Design at Imagination, an open and exploratory research lab at Lancaster University where he is also Research Director for the Lancaster Institute for the Contemporary Arts and Associate Director of the Institute for Social Futures. He lives and walks in Manchester.

Acknowledgments

Many of the ideas in *Dark Matters* were initially auditioned as talks, walks and conversations. I am grateful to the audiences, wayfarers and raconteurs who listened, shared their thoughts and gave me encouragement and feedback along the way. The original premise for this book was first presented as part of the *Sensing Architecture* symposium held at the Royal Academy of Arts in London on 29th March 2014. The enthusiastic reception for it is the root for what follows. Whilst this book is about my experiences of nocturnal urban landscapes, many of its ideas and the thinking around them were further refined through walks in the daytime and for this I am indebted to my walking companion Zola, an astute and instinctive critic. Considerable thanks are also necessary to my family and friends who have supported and been understanding of my nocturnal peregrinations over the years. Difficult circumstances in the last few years have on numerous occasions led to nightwalking being fundamental to restoring balance, living proof that amongst the darkness there is always meaning.

If I were to thank everyone who inspired or buoyed the writing of *Dark Matters*, the book and our journey into the nocturnal city together would never get started, so I will stick to the trodden path (for once) and focus only on those who provided direct help with copyrighted material or worked closely on the manuscript. Therefore, I would like to thank Julie Campbell aka LoneLady for allowing me to include her lyrics in this book, Jon Ashley and Mike Gray aka the Sov Twins for enabling me to use lyrics from The Obsession and also Rebecca Boulton for her help in gaining permission to use lyrics from Joy Division. I would also like to give my sincerest gratitude to Doug Lain for his patience during this book's production, Dominic C. James for his help along the way and Emma Jacobs for her attentive copy-editing and proofreading.

Preface

Thinking about the elusive, spectral and sometimes fleeting nature of walking through cities at night is why this book is now in front of you. Therein lies an immediate issue which rather than push into the shadows we should bring into discussion. Capturing the essence of the nocturnal city could well be an oxymoron. Antoine de Saint-Exupéry's incantation serves well here: 'Night, the beloved. Night, when words fade and things come alive. When the destructive analysis of day is done, and all that is truly important becomes whole and sound again' (1986, 10). Yet the apparent redundancy of words to ascribe explanation to and of the nocturnal city is the essential reason to engage them. The nature of the urban night and its shifting qualities is the reason why I have been compelled to write about it. However, it is within attempting to describe this fluid character that the difficulty also becomes obvious. Cities are subject to change; they are constructions and agglomerations of myriad elements. But they are also reconstructions. Cities are created, shaped and remain as much in our imagination as in hard material facts. So how to best convey the flux and fleetingness, the rip and curl of the night across the urban landscape? This book has been a while coming. In fact its very brevity has been instrumental to its delay. Numerous people I spoke to about this book during its gestation period have been fascinated by the idea of it and what it might contain. I hope they and you will not be disappointed. The desire to share some of my experiences and reasons for exploring the urban night are what follows. The sketchy origins of this book are rooted in over twenty-five years of walking around cities at night. From the outer suburbs of Greater Manchester during my teenage years; exploring the coal-mined landscape, abandoned buildings, industrial detritus and decay; to more recent encounters with international cities around the world; investi-

1

gating drastic differences and nuanced similarities, the nocturnal city has been a constant, if not always coherent, companion. There is *so* much to enjoy out there, I hope this book inspires you to do so.

Before we encounter more ideas, I would like to briefly divert the reader's attention towards the format of this book and its contents. As an entity it serves a dual purpose as it seeks to provide a proposition: a call and response to its own concepts if you will. It is therefore arranged into a series of short essays that explore different dimensions to nightwalking in cities. The first may be thought of as an introduction, which presents the strange familiarity of the nocturnal city. There follow sections on: walking, sensing, connecting and thinking. Clearly, as in life, these are not delaminated layers of being and there is much overlap between them as they shape and converse with each other. Finally, a conclusion on what I have termed a manifesto for nightwalking in cities.

Interspersed between these more analytical and theoretical texts are descriptive accounts from some of my own walks around one city. Initially, I had considered whether each one of these should be from different cities I have walked around at night. In the interests of the overall work, I made a conscious decision to draw on a number of experiences from one city, Manchester. As well as being my home city and the one with which I am most familiar, there are two main reasons for this. Firstly, no two walks at night are ever the same and those described here intersect and trace over each other, which enables me to explain the distinct differences within the composite whole. Secondly, whilst walking in new, unfamiliar cities can be a rewarding and rich experience, I wish to direct attention to the familiar and the everyday in order to extol their virtues (and of course sometimes their downright strangeness) which I believe would not be possible in the same way if multiple locations were chosen. The adjacency, rather than complete integration, of the narratives with the essays in the different sections of the book is intentional, to reinforce the connection between theory and practice whilst retaining their distinctive qualities. I hope the reader will understand and forgive this digression. It is the first of many.

Strangely Familiar

All that is solid melds into where?

Unlike promises we make to each other, the promise of the city can never be broken. But unlike the promises we hold for each other, neither can it be fulfilled.

—Victor Burgin, *Some Cities* (1996, 7)

Welcome.

What we are about to explore together is the nocturnal city. This is a place and time within which escape from the calibrations and shackles of the daytime is possible. More specifically, it is a state of *being*. Increasingly faced with infinite options of pointless choices, our ability to actually do anything meaningful seems to be exponentially disappearing. Thanks to the complex absurdities of neoliberalism, creativity and freedom of expression are left to wander about like the protagonist in *The Truman Show*, ever watched, measured and exploited, though we seldom detect it. But most importantly, they are *contained* and rarely work convincingly outside of its carapace. The acceleration of cities as *the* space within which to operate is reflected in the kaleidoscopic wormhole of economics, politics and, for the most part sanitized, culture. Capitalism's greatest achievement may reside in the urban landscapes that adorn our planet. In this sense, talking about specificity may no longer matter. We can, and some people do, discuss 'cities' and 'the urban' as if they are handheld objects; indeed this may be part of the problem. However, we also know this to be untrue. Thus, despite the increasing homogenization of different places, it is important to emphasize from the outset that cities are not neutral containers or aspatial. This may seem so obvious as to not be worth stating. But I just did, and for good reason. At a time when our encounters with the city are more mediated than ever before, it feels necessary. It is fundamental. This is because the essential qualities of our surroundings are disappearing. Urban landscapes have undergone significant transformation through their development as the context for civilization *par excellence*, a process that rapidly sped up through industrialization of cities and the subsequent predilections of neoliberal late capitalism for multivalent forms of business. The question is how and *when* to respond and break out of the dome.

In his seminal book, *All That Is Solid Melts Into Air*, Marshall

Berman argues that:

> To be modern is to live a life of paradox and contradiction... It
> is to be both revolutionary and conservative: alive to new
> possibilities for experience and adventure, frightened by the
> nihilistic depths to which so many modern adventures lead,
> longing to create and to hold on to something real even as
> everything melts. (1988, 13–14)

In this way, Berman identifies the perpetual tensions between
development and decay; the personal and the social, whilst
encouraging the wider embrace of being modernist as a means of
contemporary living. He necessarily draws upon earlier periods
of modernism, including the works of Goethe and Karl Marx, the
latter providing his book's title. However, it may be useful to
query whether the same dialectic holds for us now. Although
various claims for modernism's demise, resuscitation and legacy
continue to haunt cultural discourse, not least with respect to
architecture, the idea that it has gone and been replaced appears
erroneous. As with many cultural and stylistic developments that
inform society, modernism has been consumed and remains
partially digested in the belly of capital, awaiting occasional
bouts of flatulence. Considered in this manner, it is possible to
understand the contemporary situation as one of plurality and
diversity, wherein we are not post- anything but merely triangu-
lated by a dizzying, psychedelic array of previous cultural
identities and movements. The difference lies in their restless
ability to meld together. As such, we find ourselves consistently
presented with the 'new,' but it is typically anything but,
concocted as it is from earlier eras albeit in variegated forms. The
tensions between the will toward physical and social transformation set against the desire for physical and social stability still
exist. The significant change has been the liquidity of both
aspects since the time of Berman's writing. The endless flux of

regurgitated ideas that *appear* novel is seductive. The process of assemblage has entranced us, belying its content, succoured in the knowledge that we have not seen something before yet comforted by its familiarity as it is born from the echoes of the past. This, then, raises an important question – can we step outside of this situation to garner some much-needed perspective? Further still, if it is possible to do so, how and when might this be?

With an overwhelming amount of information and options available to us, it is extremely difficult to make a choice about what to do that may provide respite from the coopted military-entertainment-complex. Faced with this dilemma myself, I found the force field of digital technologies unhelpful as my attention slowly yielded to their tractor beam. Similarly, attempts to subvert normative practices during the daytime were highly limited whilst total abandonment was neither desirable nor practical. At night, the jumbling of ideas and problems, the half-lives of previous projects and memories all stirred deeply within. Having exhausted various approaches to counter this restlessness I decided to take to the streets, which seemed sympathetic to this disquiet. More specifically, the nocturnal city was not simply a place and time that enabled me to explore my thoughts as I walked, but became a syncopated landscape, furthering and accentuating my own rhythms both physical and psychological.

Over the last few years especially, I have spent many, many hours walking through various cities at night. The history of walking through cities is as old as that of cities themselves, and as a practice subject to a multitude of different uses and interpretations. Walking at night, however, offers something different, having the capacity to alter our ingrained, seemingly natural predispositions towards the urban surroundings, and our perceptions along with it. This has an important dual function, as this book contends. It allows the architecture of the city to be sensed differently. Architecture, through its presence and function, is typically a reflection of the values of the society that built it. Yet no matter how permanent our buildings may appear, there are temporal relationships occurring inside and outside – weathering, occupying, adapting – that subtly alter the fabric of the city. By venturing into the urban night it is possible to experience the materiality of the city as distinct from its character in the daytime. It appears somehow more porous; the shadow-play across its edifices is rich, deep and gelatinous. In addition, and perhaps of greater significance, it fosters a different way of thinking. In an age of hyper-visibility, encountering anything genuinely new seems incredibly remote, weirdly distanced from us yet at the same time ever-present and depthless. As the feedback loops on all forms of culture tighten, we seem to have reached a terminal inertia of restless regurgitation. The need for a time-place to imagine alternatives becomes increasingly urgent. Oppositional strategies such as abject despondency or rejection through nonparticipation have their potentialities but also their limitations. The appearance of eschewal may be another way forward. For within this are myriad possibilities for recalcitrance and discovery, i.e. we can give our attention to things and ideas. The point here is not necessarily *where* this occurs but *when*.

Finding oneself in the nocturnal city can be a useful aphorism. Why might this be? Cities at night are distinct, constellations of light within shadow and tempos of spectacle that contrast with the daytime. Consider the city nearest to you. Perhaps you live or work there, go out to socialize, mingle with others or attend events etc. This city is not one but has a dual character. This is the crosshatch of two cities like China Mieville's Beszél and Ul Qoma, conjoined and overlaid yet also offset from one another. We can invoke the daytime city here but much is 'unseen,' strangely familiar but also otherworldly. This uncanny character of the nighttime city squeezes and stretches place. Staccato rhythms of the day are more fluid in the nocturnal hours, the hum and drum of the urban tribe instead replaced by streams and seams of stimulation which as the hours accumulate from midnight become trickles and abandoned mines save for the semaphore of bottles, cans, fast-food wrappers and cigarette ends.

One of the first obstacles is with regard to the everyday. We can develop a tendency to think of the places we live as being the same, static or even boring. Just because something *appears* commonplace does not make it so. Surrounded by what largely look to be identical backdrops to our lives, it is easy to forget this is an environment. The psychologist James J. Gibson (1979) would describe this as a 'niche,' not to be confused with the habitat of a species – i.e. not where it lives, but rather how it lives. It is within this difference that it is easy to miss the point about how we relate to the urban landscape. There is also a further layering of the relationship. The city is not simply out *there* – a built construction separate from ourselves – but in the *here* of our bodies: its particles inhaled and exhaled; its materiality and textures informing our gait and steadily reshaping our footwear; its smells, sights and sounds comforting us or perhaps causing concern. And, of course, pertinently the *here* of our mind where we reconstruct the city many times over, forging new maps and narratives in response to its restlessness. It lives within us and us within it. The artificiality of the built environment is transformed at night, a loose third place between the natural world and the stark configuration of the daytime city. This is the nocturnal city.

For darkness has long fingers and a multitude of pockets within its cloak. When we encounter the urban night its super-natural qualities unfurl depending on the mode and speed with which we move through it. Walking is an inscriptive practice, its rhythms are incantations, finding the fissures of urban space and loosening them up, bringing forth seizures of place. This is the nighttime city, thereafter doleful and spent in the pre-dawn dimness awaiting reprisal tomorrow. The subliminal slowness of the city at night enables the urban landscape to be disinterred – clumsy histories plastered layer upon layer, increasingly disappearing remnants of yesteryear, symbols of forgotten promises, foreclosed desires and unspoken understandings. The peril is the perishable. The contemporary city is a redacted text, teeming with impoverished sentences and fraught punctuation. Overzealous editors commissioning and leading copy, previous articles shredded for noncompliance to the grand narrative. But dyslexia takes hold as the kerning of the streets is less assured and defined. Hieroglyphics are architecture's muted voice at night, incomprehensible messages jumbled together, the platen slipped and the urban type offset. Memory and the exorcism of personal notations, literal footnotes made through the passage of time and place. This renders the nocturnal city disturbing in its missive.

On the one hand it is very familiar, we recognize its streets, its architecture and its composition. Yet on the other hand we enter its strangeness, a different domain that yields its features: sometimes readily and sometimes requiring considerable excavation. This is where attention is required, an important facet of the nighttime city which we will discuss more of later. For now, it suffices to know that being *present* and *attentive* in the nocturnal city is quite different from behaviours and practices that simply extend daytime activity into the night. It also has emancipatory powers, allowing us to shake off worries of the daily grind. Leaving for tomorrow, walking at night is to make a claim for attention to be directed and maintained on the immediate environment. This is what is at stake. In the acceleration of culture, stepping outside both physically and psychologically is to reflect on a quickly eroding island of attention. Our minds are skewered. Penetrated and prone to the subconscious hauntings of unanswered emails, status updates and virtual check-ins to prove we really are not here. Our fear of missing out may lead to always being at the point of departure whenever we arrive, the constant distractions and anxieties of online profiles confused with being present. This now bristles to such an extent that the idea of being absent, to really embrace 'lack' of interference, seems like a surreal, utopian construct. Deliberately opting out of 24/7 availability, and therefore conventionally accepted accountability in the twenty-first century is a choice, albeit a very particular one. This option is especially difficult given the pervasive and mobile nature of technologies. Intrinsic to such a stance are connotations of regression, disconnection, impoliteness; all unintended signals generated through the act of doing nothing. Social media is a significant element of this composition. In a relatively short amount of time, i.e. the period in which digital networks have effaced mass communication, we have now reached a situation wherein many of us bypass actual face-to-face relationships and connections for those given by proxy. Online platforms and apps appeal to us since they suggest a lightness of touch, a never forgetting (but also never really being focused upon), 'I may not be here but I am there.' However, the cost of maintaining these 'connections' can be exhausting in many different senses, not least for our minds and attention. Where and when can we go?

Architecture may be the original situated technology, supporting social relations and connections. It is also time-bound and has a relationship to space, whether sensitive to its context, indifferent or defiant. Gleaning place from space is no mean feat. But this is what architecture does all the time for good or ill to our sense of our surroundings. At night, though, architecture's power transforms the sense of location and orientation in a very different manner. Hitherto barely detectable features take on an altogether different quality in the dark. Urban crevices, interstitial spaces and the city's margins loom forth in their confidence. The footnotes in these places are rich palimpsest, disclosing temporary inhabitation, sharp tangs of detritus and passage, dank and dripping, sunk and slippery against the more rational and acceptable materiality of the city. These charged voids of the night purr with anticipation of comings and goings, indiscriminate toward their dwellers' predilections and cravings. To be on your own in the city at night is not to be *alone*. The architecture follows you, in close conspiracy with the city's streets. Noctambulation is at odds with the contemporary city. To walk around, to enjoy the atmosphere and the ecology of the urban night, is to appear strange and questionable in the minds of others. Authoritarian figures may be even less enamored and more threatened by apparent motivelessness. 'You *must* be doing something?' Such deeply entrenched pseudo-authority must be queried.

The city, then, is on the one hand knowable but never completely captured. It eludes confinement as it reproduces itself in the mind into multiple versions, beckoning Italo Calvino's *Invisible Cities*. Interpretation of the city is how we locate ourselves and in relation to each other. We form maps based on cognition of memorable places, street names and other spatial cursors. During the nocturnal hours such cartography may be dramatically rescaled and retraced as daytime landmarks recede and new, often highly illuminated ones become signifiers instead. The beguiling effects of urban illumination tell a different story of the city. Indeed an alternative historiography for architecture could concern itself with the nighttime city. The 2014 film *Neon* directed by Eric Bednarski documents the history of urban illumination within Warsaw, political ideology wrought in glass tubes and inert gas. Whilst intentionally diverting, it is away from the bright lights we will go. Apart from the promenades and main thoroughfares, the secondary and tertiary arteries of the city are laid out under fitful incandescent filigree. Now the very materiality of the city is hewn again. Glass, duplicitous in either black mirror or virtual membrane between illuminated inside and the street outside. Stone features gurn with rugged shadows further accentuating their carved patterns and details. Brick walls, in collective planar agreement during the daytime, suddenly oust their discordances, the unsteady overhangs of mortar betraying their lack of uniformity. Metal gathers light, vagabond conductors for refracted electric bulbs. Meanwhile, the shadows refuse to conform to the allocated building plots, skewed, stretched and squeezed across facades and streets alike. A slipped mask, they fall away, loosening some edges whilst scoring sharp geometry when confronted with light source. The whole array quickly dispersed by the lights of a passing vehicle and then replenished.

The start of the night is electric with possibilities. Sodium lamps slowly warming themselves into action, wheezing phosphorous tinges dash the night sky moving from blue to inky black. The pattern-cut suburban landscape loses its edges, softening in the gloaming. Beyond the tamed and cultivated thresholds, nature runs amok – spearing the sky with charcoal tendrils, bulging through chain-link fences and aroused by the wind it rustles inward and outward, stretching its parched and tenebrous lungs. This and only this draw our attention. Not *just* this, for there is nothing absent, but the presence is everything at night. Even the things supposedly missing are keenly felt. Lack of light, dearth of vision, imbalance of senses, it all combines to form a decoupling of the daytime into something thicker, maybe heavier yet also paradoxically weightless. The mind slowly percolates the day's concerns, leaving them scattered behind, seeds in time exfoliated in the waxing and waning of the night.

After all, this is the nocturnal city…

The night stretches before me. The background slish of traffic on the Mancunian Way overhead as I emerge, walking slowly from the subway, ears prickled by the smashing of glass somewhere behind. This is Manchester on a cold and wet winter night where the opacity of the city's infrastructure loses its gravity and melds toward the neon and sodium morse code above. Indecipherable messages, these ghost texts to unknown gods and spirits hang in the air like stolen thoughts from another time – the lost future that got delayed, tied down in the bondage of bureaucracy, boredom and blame. But now the shouting is all over. Instead, this award-winning concrete serpent remains frozen against asphalt forever, undulating between buildings and woven across the landscape. My left foot skids on the masticated remains of a club flyer chewed by rain and indifference. Where now for the secret, the quiet and contemplative?

Onward and up the ramp which, glistening in the wet, looks like the runway to the Beetham Tower beyond, its red lights stretching out the astral plane of the city into something significant in height if unknown in character. The decrepit shadows of Little Ireland, Engels' long-since-vanished horror, squalid memories held in brick and mortar hang around these streets. Slinking down alongside the culverted Medlock, the repressed industrial memories of yesteryear flow underneath hundreds of sleeping students in their castle. The dank walls of the railway viaduct run to an open mouth, the archway littered with jetsam from last night's gigs and clubs, shorn from revellers in the witching hour. Geometric fungi courtesy of the street artist Truth adorn the underbelly of the arch, somewhat tarnished and stained by the weeping brickwork after rainfall.

I am now spat out into the meniscus of Whitworth Street as it bends against the Bridgewater canal. Turning right, upward to where Oxford Street and Road kiss between The Grand Old Lady and eclectic baroque of the Refuge Assurance Building, crenellated walls run down major vistas into the city. Not tonight though. Instead, a quick retrace finds me down by the water, murky grey-brown lava, sludging past unnoticed behind the blank looks of apartments and offices. Under the bridge and along the path the buildings loom inwards, a scrum of architecture leaving the constricted sky a mere navy-black bruised ribbon above.

So here I am again, a nocturnal dowser, summoning the ghostly streams of the city – palimpsestic phantoms interned in asphalt and brick lie doleful and bereft of any awakening. Flowing along the canal path, figures ahead once merged are now fleeting as new unions separate then disappear upon my footsteps. A young man with streetlamp jaundiced eyes piercing the shadows weighs up options and chances, then knocks a bottle over harrying to street level and the carn(iv)al atmosphere above. Onward and inward through the city's guts, bellicose rumblings overhead and muffled snippets of the urban corpus waft in and out of audibility. Walking down here is like sloshing through molasses save the stench – which is acrid rather than sweet – with each footstep thick as it pushes into the dark, tinged with apprehension. Slowly ascending from this underworld, I hear the stray clatter of heels and voices braying for carriages several streets away. The sterility of Piccadilly Gardens, neutered public space at its most banal, nullifies thought and reflection. Engulfed in stone and turf platitudes even the typically lachrymose fountains can shed no more at this hour. The eels of the tramlines course in studied curvature towards Shudehill, but the gravity of Market Street draws the feet down its incline toward the pillar box at Corporation Street. That open-mouthed witness to the IRA bomb on 15 June 1996 no longer silently screaming in red but quietly memorialized in gold. Here the burnished image of the city in the aftermath of restoration and pre-millennial development can only reflect back its own emptiness. To my right, the reconstituted Sinclair's Oyster Bar and The Old Wellington Inn, themselves not saved from the traditional butchery that once resided here, now grafted together perpendicular to one another.

The downward pull continues over the River Irwell, that molten mirror that both divides and stitches Manchester and Salford. The ancestral home of Celts and Romans long since passed through, the landscape at this hour has a meagre and disparate tribe of weary pleasure-seekers, looking for the embers of another party with just a few cigarette fireflies to animate their own waggle dance. Turning left down Chapel Street, Suprematist sculptures of light pin down roller shutters, bins and fences. Furtive side streets back away into the shadows, the cold air palpable and heavy in my lungs. Fragmented and resuscitated post-war dreams of inner-city ring roads sweep my direction back toward the city with its four-lane impasse but it cannot compete with the punctuated industrial rhythms of the Victorian railway hulking onward to my right. The arches, far from being voids, seem to be moulds for urban aspic; holding detritus, snuffling sounds, papers and plastics in a choreomania beyond my translation. It must be past 5am by now, time to head home through sodium-fused suburbs.

Walking:

Opening up the fissures of the city at night

In wide arcs of wandering through the city
I saw to either side of what is seen,
and noticed treasures where it was thought there were none.
I passed through a more fluid city.
I broke up the imprint of familiar places,
shutting my eyes to the boredom of modern contours.

—A. A. Dun, *Vale Royal* (1995)

The containment of ideas within the city is subtle. Urban landscapes are typically dynamic entities: diverse spaces and flows where culture, commerce and communities appear to effortlessly interact and *produce*. The dome of capitalism within which such activity is protected also calcifies the very same. Limitless growth is impossible without reproduction. Without originality and innovation the only trajectory possible is via inward spiralling paths toward repetition, renovation and reprise. In the city the *remix* is paramount. But also within the city, there are cracks: both material and temporal. Harder to gauge in the daytime within the confines of routine, at night they may be more easily sensed. For, even in the twenty-first century, our attempts to metricize time and space have not fully converted the nocturnal city into the daytime landscape of production. At least not yet, but the ambition is there in precariat, zero-hour contracts, just-in-time 24/7 operations, and the transposition of always-on digital networks to the physical environment. No rest for the wicked indeed, not when we can spend money and others make it. So, how best to slip through the mesh? One potential place is the nocturnal city since it provides a discrete time during which creativity may flourish and ideas may be nurtured. In order to give our ideas full attention the distractions of transportation systems, whether public or private, are an unwelcome diversion. This is a landscape for walking.

To engage with the nocturnal city, it is important to consider what walking provides as a means of exploring cities. The key aspect of walking is that it directly connects us to our surroundings in a manner other forms of mobility do not. At a period in human history when so much of our activity is uploaded, categorized, tagged and compressed into moments, I contend that to sense a wider and deeper world candidly through first-hand encounter becomes more important than ever. Stepping, quite literally, out of the glare and stare of our structured and commoditized days and into alternative modalities within the shadows of our cities may be one of the few truly sublime and beautiful urban practices left to us.

Walking, then, nothing more but certainly nothing *less*. Journeys and travails of the night have been the subject of contemporary depictions (Sandhu 2007) whilst walking as a methodology has recently been reclaimed by artists, writers and architects (Sinclair 1997, Careri 2001). Concomitant with this, much has been made of psychogeography and various attempts to exhume the spirit of the Situationists. This is not a problem in itself. But it is a limitation, chiming with our ever-growing need to classify and label so it can be curated online, shared and liked. It is a very lazy shorthand if not completely moribund trope within which to collect a plurality of voices and practices that are often distinctly diverse and fine in detail. This perhaps says considerably more about the way we are increasingly made to perceive cities as homogenized amalgamations of capital accumulation and market forces rather than as places. Indeed, even outside of such discourse there is much romance ascribed to nighttime peregrinations, the disclosure of surreptitious operations and liminal actors, yet the reality often experienced is bound up in regulation and control. Indeed as the cultural geographer Tim Edensor has noted, when we walk through cities we are expected to *conform*. This means we moderate the speed, direction and expression of our bodies in motion in response to both the built environment and the people around us. To run, to leap, or to move in any way erratically is to warrant suspicion. How did this spatial practice that has huge potential to be stimulating become so banal?

Part of this is to do with the complex, although somewhat depleted, status walking has seemingly arrived at in our twenty-first century lives. Walking is an innate human process; on a practical level it is how we move ourselves through space, previously allowing our ancestors to go in search of food (or a mate) or to evade a predator. Yet the basic necessity of walking is also supplemented by choice and the way it facilitates us to negotiate our relationship with place. In his history of walking, Joseph Amato (2004) draws a parallel between the development of human activity and its primary form of motion – whether as migrations, pilgrimages, pleasure or protest – as an essential part of our being present in the world and connecting with our surroundings. In fact, walking is so elemental to our being that that we seldom think to even question its broader attributes and implications. There are perhaps some pretty straightforward explanations for this prevailing situation. We typically learn to walk from an early age and as such the act is swiftly normalized – when walking we are pedestrian as both noun *and* adjective. The additional definition of 'pedestrian' is unfortunate here, because of its tendency to lead us to subconsciously connect notions of the commonplace and dull with going on foot, as opposed to the perceived glamour and excitement of travelling by car, for example. This mundane experience of walking is, though, a familiar one, especially in the daytime when we might be moving between errands or within time constraints such as popping to the shops in our lunch hour. Yet, amidst the ever-accelerating velocity of contemporary culture and society with all its attendant distractions it is no surprise that to walk without a specific purpose or destination in mind can feel substantial or instrumental enough to function as a twenty-first-century urban practice.

Even in these situations and in overtly stimulating environments such as cities, walking can still sometimes appear repetitious and monotonous – but, I would argue, it is never boring. The philosopher Frédéric Gros provides a clear distinction of the difference between monotony and boredom. Writing about states of wellbeing, he explains:

The accursed peculiarity of pleasure, very often discussed, is that repetition reduces its intensity. The good object that has fulfilled me can be consumed with renewed pleasure a second time, perhaps even more intensely because, being prepared, I adopt a posture of *appreciation*: I try to explore every dimension, to taste it in all its fullness. A third time, a fourth... by now the furrows, the ruts, are already traced, and it becomes something known, or recognized. (2014, 14)

There are, of course, myriad aspects to a city; so many and some changing so rapidly that it is impossible to explore all of them in their fullness. Perhaps the recent compulsion to collect fragmentary experiences of the real world, subsequently shared online, may be seen as a tactic to respond to this sheer, overwhelming vastness. This somewhat misses an opportunity for mental and physical release. It is this very capacity of cities, to be continuously piquing our curiosity and inviting our inspection, that makes them so fertile for both physical and psychological exploration. As Walter Benjamin noted: 'Not to find one's way in a city may well be uninteresting and banal. It requires ignorance—nothing more. But to lose oneself in a city— as one loses oneself in a forest—that calls for quite a different schooling' (1978, 8–9). In Benjamin's terms, to be lost is to be fully present, and to be fully present is to be capable of revelling in uncertainty and mystery. Extending this discussion in her book *Wanderlust*, Rebecca Solnit explores the profound relationship between thinking and walking, walking and culture, and argues for the preservation of the time and space in which to walk in an ever-more car-dependent and accelerated world. As she explains:

to make walking into an investigation, a ritual, a meditation, is a special subset of walking, physiologically like and philo-sophically unlike the way the mail carrier brings the mail and the office worker reaches the train... The imagination has both shaped and been shaped by the spaces it passes through on two feet. (2000, 3–4)

So, if we think about the history of humanity as also being in essence the history of cities, albeit played out across a very long timeframe, where does this leave us in the twenty-first century? The nature of this chronicle has become increasingly relevant as more and more of us live, work and play within urban landscapes. Cities are very much at the top of many govern-ments' agendas. They are also often viewed as the supreme sites of culture, commerce and capital. But parallel to this obvious account of our existence is an alternative history: the story of our relationship with the night, our fears, struggles and perceptions of the dark; our attempts to vanquish it and ultimately conquer our environment through illumination, to exert artificial and manmade control over circadian rhythms. There is a long history of night travels as integral to 'cultures of darkness' (Palmer 2000) that also reveals distinct relationships between writing and walking (Beaumont 2015). These are frequently depicted as shady worlds of miscreants, shift workers and transgressors. Yet the night offers much to be enjoyed beyond vice. Night by definition contrasts day, summoning notions of darkness and fear. But another night exists out there, providing escape from daily routine. Liberation and exhilaration in the margins of the city are increasingly rare when the prevailing fluidity of consumptive experience has smoothed our time-space relationships with multivalent forms of commoditization (Bauman 2000). Rather than consider darkness as negative, oppositional with illumi-nation and enlightenment, we need to explore the rich potential of the dark, or perhaps more precisely the never-quite-dark, of the nocturnal city as an alternative frame for thinking and being.

Scan the bestseller lists and airport lounges and the widespread interest in cities is in plain view. Whether as places for happiness (Montgomery 2013), wealth (Glaeser 2011), social cohesion (Minton 2009) or positive transformation (Hollis 2013) the burgeoning arena of discourse and mainstream media in recent years has cast them to the forefront of public consciousness. Cities have long been considered the nexus of culture, commerce, community and society. More recently, however, they have become the new ground for a different and frequently much more subtle type of exploitation. This has manifested as a construct for venture capitalists, economists, politicians and corporations amongst others to recalibrate the failing rhetoric of accelerated neoliberal capitalism into a more fluid, pervasive and insidious site for business. The message is clear if not explicitly tattooed across the built environment: if you are not consuming you are not welcome. The failure of the market to deliver continued growth has brought with it the much-vaunted thousand blooms but these are thorny, germinated under the guise of creative classes, gentrification and greater coagulation of wealth for too few. At a time when the entire urban environment is mapped, recorded, indexed and classified to saturation point at which discovery is bound to a monitor and reality yields little new experience, it may be the everyday that provides some respite and recuperation from such forces. More threatening to the nocturnal city are the continued attempts to pervade it with the same strategies that make it open for business, a mere extension of the day. Rather than being a time and place for dormancy, reflection and consideration it is rapidly becoming engulfed in the market. It was not always this way. The nighttime city was understood through various periods to be a considerable problem, the ultimate haunting ground for the desperately sad, bad or mad.

Indeed, the threat of night has also been legislated against; as a cover it has been historically assailed by the intrusions of light (Schivelbusch 1995), and more recently the proliferation of technologies illuminating its dark corners and opening it up to the glare and stare of surveillance and scrutiny. Toward the end of the twentieth century, Jean Baudrillard would summarize the disappearing invasion of the night in terms of universalizing loss, the bland homogenizing of humanity and history thus:

Ours is rather like the situation of the man who has lost his shadow: either he has become transparent, and the light passes right through him or, alternatively, he is lit from all angles, overexposed and defenceless against all sources of light. We are simultaneously exposed on all sides to the glare of technology, images and information, without any way of refracting their rays; and we are doomed in consequence to a whitewashing of all activity – ...social relations, bodies, memories... (1993, 44)

Our history with darkness over the centuries suggests quite a different story. Despite the accumulation of such measures to counter the perceived impending nightly devastations, the night did not typically bring forth ominous, even fatal, clashes of uncompromising individuals or groups but enabled more discretely clandestine histories. These were vital times, places and spaces where human expression was not as easily subjected to the scrutiny of daytime. Modest but highly valued freedoms from the bonds and worries of daily life could be found here. This is a history that seldom leaves traces so it is worth us briefly delving into the past to understand some of the origins of our attitudes toward darkness.

In contrast to our contemporary view of it, in the past, rather than falling, night was understood to rise. As Ekirch has noted, the 'darkness of the night appears palpable. Evening does not arrive, it "thickens"' (2005, xxxi). This smothering of the landscape as the firmament of night condensed provides understanding as to perhaps why it has sometimes been referred to as man's first necessary evil, our oldest and most haunting terror. In his 1757 treatise, *A Philosophical Enquiry into the Origin of Our Ideas of the Sublime and Beautiful*, Edmund Burke claimed that darkness remained, as always, 'terrible in its own nature.' Throughout history, the nocturnal accomplice of darkness has cast the shadowy hours of evening and early morning as a time and space during which our rational thought could be circumvented by fear, our understanding of routine and environment be skewered by transgressions, and our innermost sanctums be invaded by unwanted guests, imaginary or sometimes deadly real. So where now for the secret, the contemplative, the quiet and subterranean? The question may no longer be what types of spaces we wish to engage with or even where they are located but *when* are they?

To return to one of the positions of this book outlined earlier, the primacy of architecture is perhaps not its body in light but the itinerant, fleeting shawl of darkness. In the nocturnal city the built environment recasts our senses away from the visual. We are less confident in our ability to see at night and place greater reliance on multi-sensory feedback, all the while trying to keep our fears in abeyance. Beyond the seemingly omnipotent eye of CCTV cameras and security measures, gestures of refusal to accept the accessible, banal versions of the urban landscape proffered by platforms such as Google Street View appear evident in the visceral and insightful practice of nightwalking. To clarify my intentions here, I am not interested in drawing further attention and discussion to the bacchanalian and ribald behaviour and events that we may easily associate with nights out in cities. Sensational as they may be, they arguably do little more than to provide further diversion from something more essential with regard to the experience of us in the nocturnal city. Furthermore, they also add more weight to the idea of the city as only an arena of consumption, which is both limited and calcifying for the purposes of our thinking about alternatives.

The liminal landscape of the nocturnal city is an intersection of the physical and psychological state of being present. Away from the major thoroughfares, the nighttime city is an extension of the nightwalker as the buildings are buttoned up and the streets zip together to form long, sinewy paths with scarce activity. The interregnum between day and night flows steadily and permeates all in its wake. Various writers have sought to comprehend this 'world without a name' in order to understand the strange life hidden in the darkness of the city. As Bressani, writing about Balzac's Paris and the introduction of gaslight to the city, describes:

> It is no longer the world of insurgents and criminals but of a life radically *other* where the natural laws that govern daily life are no longer valid. As much as light contrasts its fairy magic to fetid obscurity, darkness reclaims its mystery facing the flood of light of the boulevards. There is a phantasmagoria of light, just as there is a phantasmagoria of darkness. One engenders the other, but each has its own character. (2015, 33)

The promulgation of the idea of darkness as the harbinger of fear was well established prior to the introduction of artificial lighting in cities, though the increased urban life that populated hitherto darkened hours brought it back into the public conscious. There is certainly an element to walking at night that has a close kinship to the ethos of wandering but for it to be solely this would be to suggest it is far more aimless and meandering than it often is. To go out walking into the nocturnal city is a decisive act. In the ever-accelerating velocity of contemporary society with all its attendant distractions, we are strangely rendered impotent toward creating the new. The accompanying ability for the folds of time and culture to exhaust themselves in Möbius strips of bricolage, pastiche and diminishing significance simply reinforces this neutralization. Far from cooperating with the commodification of the city at night, it can be subtly resisted. This may not, necessarily, be the purview of collective action.

Moving around cities in groups may be very difficult without official sanction, the right to protest becoming an increasingly limited act in real time due to dispersal zones and policing strategies and then the subsequently poorly reported version, with little fidelity to the passion and position of those involved. There has been a growth of banned zones in cities within which people may be disbanded, moved on or even prosecuted for actions that would be widely understood as public and convivial, or certainly not assumed to be criminal, including but not restricted to: dog walking, leafleting and gathering in what may feel like moderate numbers. Walking alone at night can also be subject to circumspection and suspicion. The seemingly unnatural, questionable and alien qualities of something so simple readily replay in our mental kaleidoscope of fear-crime-horror endless combinations of bad things that could happen. But of course they very rarely do and our thoughts are typically our own worst chimera. Dreams arrive in a conscious state when nightwalking. The body and the mind are in tandem: they are *doing* things. But, unlike a gadget on standby mode, in the nocturnal city it is possible to be ever alert and deeply attentive to new emergent concepts. This correlates with the slackness of time in the nocturnal city.

Time here is elastic and foggy. The structure and metrics of daytime wax and wane in the darkness, with its ambivalence to form and accountability instead replaced by something much more fluid and less structured. Beyond the confines of daily tasks there is the emergence of a desire to claim back the night, away from the data deluge of email accounts, social-media prods and attention-leeching digital devices, toward the experiential qualities of the *here* and *now* rather than the tenuous and distant. Patrick Keiller cements the loss of our important and interwoven relationships with the urban landscape:

> Instead, in the UK and elsewhere, cities might now be distinguished not so much by the merits of their spatial form, their society, culture, and so on, but by how successfully they negotiate continual social, economic and technological change. (2013, 135)

Therefore, rather than having any room and time to create and develop new ideas and alternatives, we end up in an endless cycle of coping and then responding to unwanted change usually presented to us as an 'opportunity.' This is also known as resilience but against what exactly? Everything that voracious late capitalism can bring in its wake.

Spatial conventions and rules are relaxed if not completely abandoned as night falls. The appropriation of urban space occurs in the deep pockets of the city away from natural surveillance or the 'scanscape' of CCTV cameras. New rhythms slowly build as the impetus for claiming nocturnal margins spreads across the urban landscape. The palimpsest of the city's surfaces is added to with tags, throw-ups and pieces whilst the furtive glances buried in deep cowls elicit the adrenaline pump of those who, at least during these hours, are flowing along the edges of normative society. Bankable Banksy and his ilk have no space here. This is the reserve of those whose talents lie outside of the logics of the market. Pure expression of invisible urban networks: 'I am here and we were there.' Elsewhere, the trundle and scrape of skateboarders repurposing the city's edges and BMX bandits coalescing into their own nocturnal peloton of dispute and turf control. The corporeal bump and grind against other people's claims within the urban night is part of the unknown. Mysterious and codified, the general rule of foot is to not get embroiled in someone else's game. Amongst my own experiences, the incidence of negative encounter has been extremely rare (once in more than several hundred outings) and even the energy of that dissipated swiftly when it was apparent I was just *out there*. No urban seer or vigilante, I walk at night to think and vice versa. For me the escape of daily roles and responsibilities is to enter the melding city, slowly but perceptibly shifting its composition and character in the play of shadows. This place and time enables both the meditation on and mediation with the nocturnal city.

Alexandra Park runs alongside my steps. The landscape beyond the railings is currently undergoing restorative treatments. To go back in time to its former glories of ovals and curves when it first sought to tempt men from drinking dens. Housing shuttles by either side until the swoop toward the dual carriageway where large sheds bulldoze into view. Straggling through commercial and business parks, the night traffic in and out of the city below. To my right, a delicate metal ribbon arcs over the four-lane vehicle valley. The Epping Walk Bridge, where Joy Division were framed and shot by Kevin Cummins in snow-kissed January 1979 thereby assembling the band's (and, for a time, Manchester's) enduring myth of black-and-white post-industrial desolation. Hornchurch Court, one of the few surviving towers in Hulme, faces up to the scene of post-war demolition, the infamous if short-lived project of The Crescents. Name checking a role-call of great architects – Adam, Barry, Kent and Nash – if not living conditions, these streets in the sky were quickly abandoned by families and provided fertile compost for culture and communities when there was a real alternative. All gone. Now the unfettered expansion of the city's universities smudges its way off the education corridor and into inner-city neighbourhoods.

All Saints and hallowed ground for wandering spirits: usually animated by the hubbub of students and gig-goers. Not around here tonight though. There is no one save for those swaddled silently in the bus shelter. Manchester Art School's past of Adolphe Valette, L. S. Lowry and Ossie Clark pay silent tribute. The former's Impressionist paintings borne of the city's early-twentieth-century industrial haze catch subdued colours in their murk; the shadows and sodium lamps of the city's streets doing much the same over a century later. Grosvenor Street is a rich seam of partying archaeology. On the corner, the old picture house, Roman-Corinthian flourishes of the Renaissance, resplendent in green and cream, then the Deaf (& Dumb) Institute and at the other end the former Man Alive club-cum-shack. Venturing across Princess Street and alone amidst multiple thoroughfares is uncanny. To the right, a pure avenue to the south of the city: Victoria

Park and Fallowfield. To the left the Mancunian Way slices the night sky with its elevated poise. From this side, it is effortless geometry, gathering the arteries of the city into its weave and flow. On the other side, however, an awkward, jabbing stump points toward the city centre: a botched miscalculation, clumsily obscured by advertisement hoarding rather than celebrated. It is in details such as this that the city reveals itself. Striding into the Brunswick Estate, undergoing facelifts at present, domino blocks in attendance: perpendicular and rectangular in defiance to their surroundings.

Ardwick Green. Back against the city centre now as the Hyde Road siphons the feet upwards. On my right the former Apollo Theatre, Art Deco host to many a silver-screen icon and more latterly musicians. The changing prefixes of buildings such as this, whether breweries or mobile-network operators, are the real signs of the times. As the bold masses of bus depots, mills and warehouses slowly release the pavement line, the landscape breaks away either side. Arterial roads such as this can be indistinctive. Almost readymade, implanted strips of budget Americana: retail sheds, petrol stations, neon signs and billboards. We are not in Kansas anymore Toto. Idling off the main road toward Belle Vue where a century and a half's worth of cacophonous programming from yesteryear is buried. Zoological gardens; rollercoasters; the annual circus; and rugby league: mismatched spectaculars for all ages and tastes. All of these have eventually disappeared whilst greyhounds, motorcycle speedway, bangers and stock cars now loop the site ad nauseum.

More big sheds and lights on the carriageway. Closed fast-food outlets with chicken-fried greasy air, feet also involuntarily speed up to be fast away from the rupture of traffic still shooting down here, red hyphens of car brake lights dash the engine noise around speed cameras. Time to get off the main vein again. Winding along suburban streets the noise gradually diminishes and houses previously framing the view stop suddenly to reveal Sunny Brow Park, oasis amongst pattern-cut housing and asphalt. Bundled down amidst the trees and gently undulating landscape is Gore Brook. This valley is unusual in its semi-

rural qualities compared to other urban parks. Edging along the occasionally glistening water is the only way to go. The bank yields to the boots, unsteady and sinking into the soft dark. Vast, irregular mirrors of cloud lie beyond my feet. The smooth landscape of Gorton Reservoirs: a diptych of silvery grey-blue glass. Up on the brow of one of the edges, the night sky is temporarily held in the water, silently slinking past. Unstoppable. A perfect time and place to reflect.

Sensing:

Mediating and meditating the urban

To the centre of the city where all roads meet, waiting for you,
To the depths of the ocean where all hopes sank, searching for
you

—Joy Division, *Shadowplay* (1979)

To be in a city is usually to be surrounded by life, the urban buzz of people, traffic, sights, sounds, smells and tastes all combine within the superorganism. Unlike a static backdrop, frozen, or an empty vessel awaiting activity, the city wraps around and passes through you as its heady concoction pulls you into its rhythms, patterns and signals. During the daytime, cities may fizz with energies and exigencies, stirring the body within its soup and conforming it to within acceptable movements and behaviours. Anything and everything seems possible. But it is not. All is not as it initially appears to be. You don't need to look around for long for the signifiers of control and coercion to instruct you. Metal plate and plastic diktats applied on the city's surfaces telling us what to do, typically by virtue of informing us what *not* to do.

DO NOT RUN. NO BALL GAMES. NO SKATEBOARDING. NO LITTERING. NO LOITERING. ANTI-SOCIAL BEHAVIOUR WILL NOT BE TOLERATED. NO-ALCOHOL ZONE. NO SMOKING. NO VAPING. NO DOGS EXCEPT GUIDE DOGS. ONLY FOOD OR DRINK BOUGHT HERE MAY BE CONSUMED HERE. BIKES ATTACHED TO THESE RAILINGS WILL BE REMOVED. THE MANAGEMENT RESERVES THE RIGHT TO REFUSE ENTRY. SHOPLIFTERS WILL BE PROSECUTED. THESE PREMISES ARE SECURITY MARKED USING A DNA SYSTEM. CCTV IS IN OPERATION FOR YOUR SAFETY AND SECURITY. SMILE, YOU ARE ON CAMERA.

These boundaries seek to promote and protect certain ways of being in the city whilst explicitly demarcating and prohibiting other forms. This in turn establishes a collective subconscious of normative behaviours and actions that we tacitly accept through an osmosis-like process purely by being in the city. However, at night a strange transaction takes place. As the very edges of these boundaries become fuzzier and more porous, the enforcement is often much more forceful. The penetrating geometries of surveillance camera cones of vision, the illuminated yet empty office blocks and shops assume blocks of light that are unassailable, the public realm carefully scribed to engender adherence and conformity. But these city limits are plastic, difficult to truly enforce and based upon the servile collective's 'social' contract to not gather in too large a group, not to be too unusual, not to make too much noise or be too eerily quiet either. Perturbation urbanism at its most potent, we are steered away from freedom of expression lest we be caught in the surreptitious force fields of expenditure, passive consumption and capsular space. The interdependency between body and space did not escape the attention of Henri Lefebvre, who noted:

> the whole of (social) space proceeds from the body, even though it so metamorphoses the body that it may forget it altogether – even though it may separate itself so radically from the body as to kill it. The genesis of a far-away order can be accounted for only on the basis of the order that is nearest to us – namely, the order of the body. Within the body itself, spatially considered, the successive levels constituted by the senses (from the sense of smell to sight, treated as different within a differentiated field) prefigure the layers of social space and their interconnections. (1991, 405)

What is this faraway order and how might we get there? In the context of this book, this seemingly distant alternative may be understood as a new conception for thinking. It is one that is immediately *with* us and, exactly because of this proximity, has a mobility and durability that makes it flexible and instrumental for thinking about things away *from* us. To expand upon this notion a little further, it is the ongoing conversation between the body and the city that may enable us to question current approaches and think how best to implement alternatives. An ideal place for this is the nocturnal city since it offers respite from daily production and recuperation for ideas. It is these restorative qualities that are essential to enjoying the freedom of thought that nightwalking promotes.

One of the key points here is the disappearance of the nocturnal city as it undergoes processes to comprehensively absorb it within the rules and regulations that make cities so successful during the day. These concerns have occupied the work of Paul Virilio, who dedicated four of his most influential essays to the ongoing shift of the matter of the city into light. These texts examine the motives behind what he terms the 'rise of the false days of technoculture' wherein we are forced to accept the 'ultracity' of physiological abject and total displacement. It is the first of these essays, *The Big Night*, which we shall examine further here. This text focuses on the loss of purpose for circadian rhythms and natural light in cities. The proliferation of what he terms 'night tables' – screens and consoles, to which we may add smartphones which were not in widespread circulation at the time of his essay – suggests a fundamental switch. Through our technological roaming, on the internet or otherwise, we are supplanting a very real sociocultural need to explore the physical world and give it our attention. In fact even if we are awake at night, it is a zombie state, 'an absolute reversal of biological cycles, with inhabitants dozing by day, awake at night' (Virilio 2000, 4). This is not a state of being in polar opposition to the daytime but a more nuanced version of it. As we are complicit in this transformation, Virilio observes that: 'by freeing ourselves from natural lighting (from cosmological time), we have, in just over two centuries, come to resemble moles roaming in a *beam of light*, moles whose view of the world does not indeed amount to much' (7). Here we can understand the complexity of the situation. It is not that we are unaware of what is changing even if we are unable to sense how pervasively, subtly and fully it is shifting. More problematic is an inability to stop ourselves: data obesity as urban pandemic and substitute for a real connection with our environment and those around us. Perhaps to fully appreciate what we are losing it is more helpful to think of what and when we might benefit from it.

If we close ourselves down to the nocturnal city, favouring instead the simulacra of representations of life through digital devices, then we are condoning the elimination of the fragile physical aspects of our world that are essential to our reading of it. At night cities condense, activity drains away from its non-vital nocturnal organs and a new cartography is overlaid with the arteries bulging toward each eddy of neon-glass-sound-clash. In this semi-torpor the body of the city is a cyborg. Artificial machinations of dry ice and mirrors, U.V. lights and multi-screen security eyes resuscitate inanimate daytime spaces into *the* places as their pulse quickens to 120 beats per minute and beyond. Clubs, bars, restaurants, casinos, massage parlours and other pleasure spaces announce their presence in the city through neon signage, leaking disco lights, throbbing bass sounds and solemn security staff ready to assess attire and worth for admission. Elsewhere, the city contracts in silhouettes and reflected electric lights. Night workers that service the city etch across it systematically. In their wake they leave polished floors, guarded voids, emptied bins, buffed walls and burnished streets. The ghosts of a day's work and play are all but exorcised once more. These figures and operations are conducted in a professional trance oblivious to the causes of their quarry. The general absence of people is an uncanny experience in the urban night. A strange sensation builds up initially at their dearth, especially when someone does appear – what are their intentions, why are they here, perhaps they are the same as me, am I now in danger – a double helix of anxiousness and relief at being aware you are now no longer alone all the time bonded together by the presence of being on the streets. The 'other' is a familiar trope in literature, and indeed many forms of art and culture, concerning the city, whilst the unspeakable krakens that are aroused by fear at night become unmanageable in our logic.

The sepulchral qualities of parts of the city at night provide the perfect immersive environment for such haunting thoughts. The deep edifices of older buildings may not be found in the more recent tributes to the sky; bland lanterns of steel and glass that give nothing to the street but the emptiness of your own eyes looking back. No shelter to be sanctioned here, in favour of clean lines and minimal geometry – the curtain wall/call for the final fall of public man. This is where the glossy twenty-first-century city resides; the CGI architecture of financially blown glass, ineffable in its pointlessness. To critique such endeavour is to accept the foreclosure of architectural ambition as a stalemate of greed and hedge-fund portfolios. An unattainable zenith of commercial gain, immediately rendered obsolete upon construction, in any civic sense, for once embodied *in concreto* the idea unlike the stock exchange is predictable and flightless. Unlike time passed in the nocturnal city it is dead on arrival.

For space and time bind together at night barely distinguishable from one another. This is the chronotope that Mikhail Bakhtin (1981) posited in literary theory but in three dimensions. Not the simulated city and its multiple representations but the actual *place*. Both elements of space and time are fused together to form a viscous agent that simultaneously holds the body whilst acquiescing to its preternatural dispositions. Now the city is here with you, beside you, behind you, its datum and weight oscillating with each footstep. Oneiric rather than heroic, nocturnal outings in the urban landscape can be haunting and indescribable. Nighttime stragglers in the etiolated city go about their ways. The agency of the nocturnal city is a skeleton key to past, present and futures. It allows the unlocking of the city at night to reveal its latent energies and jewels. Solipsistic affirmation through encounter with its streets and facades, the night is the encomium to our dreams and desires. But that would suggest the city at night's countenance to such activity. Walking at nighttime can clearly raise very different perceptions of the same activity during the daylight hours, along with its protagonists and their motives. Night travels throughout history were entrenched with circumspection and disorder – a view of the night perhaps best exemplified in Brassaï's *Paris de Nuit* (1933). The industrialization of cities in the nineteenth century, especially the arrival of gas and subsequently electric lamps, forced a fundamental re-evaluation of previous prevailing attitudes to night. New requirements and new attitudes towards the night prompted attempts to vanquish the dark and ultimately conquer our environment through illumination, exerting artificial control over circadian rhythms. As urban life began more and more to populate the hitherto darkened life, nighttime entered the public conscious as a specific time and space, a nameless world that brought forth ominous feelings. Despite the measures that in many ways have made the nocturnal city safe we have retreated, folding in on ourselves in online domains. This is an oversight if not a terrible mistake.

In our era of ever-more rapid technological development the deep-seated connections we have to our urban landscapes – which sustain our relationships to the city, over and above purely economic ties – are at a real risk of being lost. The abundance of information available and presented on a portable screen, telling us where to go, what to do, who to meet, and the pervasive data networks that serve them, act to mediate our relationship to the city, distancing us from its physical and, to some degree, psychological realities. In order to reclaim some of what is being lost, it is contended here that walking into the night offers the means of exfoliating the worries and weight of familiar roles and responsibilities. This is not the chest-beating, public declaration of protest as commonly understood and which should play an important part in the vibrant city and its people. By contrast, this is a gently recalcitrant act against the confines of the daily grind. As someone for whom walking at night provides respite from the progressively attention-splicing nature of the daylight hours, to venture into the 'thickness' of the night, and go beyond its apparently opaque limits, is to sense, in a powerful and visceral way, the experiential diversity of a much broader world than that which exists during the daytime.

What, then, might the possibilities afforded by walking at night be beyond individual psychological emancipation? Recent years have seen lines drawn across many of our urban landscapes: previously tangible city limits hewn in stone, set in concrete, and now joined by invisible ones scanned by cameras. Meanwhile, the digital panopticon of CCTV and other surveillance technologies ensures those same landscapes are mapped, recorded and classified almost out of existence. Perhaps there really is nothing new to be found in urban spaces that are being rendered increasingly inert due to the acceleration of security, control and the insatiable appetite of commerce. Yet we know this is not the case. We can feel it out *there*. It is, though, not just cities that are changing, but us too. Increasing demands on our attention skew and stretch time. Leisure time as indistinct from work time – arguably one of capitalism's finest constructs – is being constantly sucked into an internet wormhole: work emails penetrating outside office hours; 24/7 concentration required for our always-on and always-connected existence; just-in-time delivery lifestyles encroaching effortlessly into our evening and night. The old crutch of recuperation and 'temporary social distance' (Melbin 1987, 123) that the nocturnal hours used to provide is now little more than a matchstick, worn down by instant and incessant communication, 140-character epistles and the fear of missing out.

Given both the sometimes subtle yet almost always pernicious changes being made to our cities, and the constant and increasingly commercialized demands on our attention, it may be seriously questioned whether most of us have the time or inclination to engage with a sense of place anymore. But, as I am trying to show, out there beyond our homes, an alternative, liminal habitat awaits us in the nocturnal city. What if we turn our attention toward the experiential qualities of the *here* and *now* in our immediate surroundings rather than the tenuous and distant? To go out walking into the night is a deliberate act – one that allows us to feel present, and connect with our surroundings in a potentially profound and meaningful way. As Bergson states: 'Though all of the photographs of a city taken from all points of view indefinitely complete one another, they will never equal in value that dimensional object, the city along whose streets one walks' (2012, 134).

This is exactly the point of apparent purposelessness. That we can go and enjoy our urban landscape without recourse to purchase or online activity, the digital umbilical cord disconnected at least for a while. Initially strange, quickly absorbing. This is the city of the imagination laid over the topography of manufacture, commerce and consumerism. Our bodies become translators between the two cities, decoding and reinventing with each footstep. Delving into the urban night is to rediscover the nocturnal palimpsest of the city. Overlaid texts of the built environment, semi-permanent markers of progress and culture. But of equal importance to the reading of the city itself is the physiological alteration. For the night brings with it personal transformation alongside that of the city, as our identities blur and shift, different traits simultaneously folding in and unfurling in relation to the tenebrous environment. Our internal weather system changes, increasingly attuned and tethered to our immediate surroundings. Out *there* is the endless possibility of night stretching out in every direction, in *here* the varying thoughts and emotions gently ebb and flow around in response to the body's changing isotherms and sensations.

The crepuscular fabric of cities has featured in many fictional narratives, but it is an essential part of our lived experience too. Streets can become supernatural and even magical at night, can appear otherworldly and beyond any pressing social concerns, gilded by the glow of streetlamps. We have all seen and even been in such places without truly breathing them in, allowing them to permeate the body and our thoughts. Rather than being daunted by the penumbra of the built environment, walking into the night can be a potentiating refractory act against the restraints of daily chores, a means of dissipating the concerns and heft of familiar roles and responsibilities. Even in those parts of the city with the greatest light pollution, the absence of people can be a strange and exhilarating experience. This is when we are most able to engage all our senses with the city. That is not to say that you always need to be alone. On a short visit to Seoul a couple of years ago, its permanent neon aura coupled with jetlag led me down by the Cheonggyecheon public park. This is a relatively recent development that replaced the highway that bifurcated the district and covered the original stream that ran there. As well as fostering natural habitat, improving cooling of neighbouring areas and increasing the uptake of public transportation, the park has also put significant numbers of the city's inhabitants and visitors back in touch with darkness. Whilst some areas along the waterway were well lit, considerable stretches were not. Families, young couples, elderly groups and solitary walkers from a broad demographic all wandered along, enjoying the night air and coursing water as it streamed past.

Our reliance on visual perception is overrated in the city. Many of us have no doubt experienced near-collisions with other pedestrians as they are focused on the device in their hand rather than the world around them, a situation further exacerbated by the addition of headphones. This kind of retreat into oneself provides even greater delineation between the city and its people. Our lack of attention to the immediate environment is driven by our belief that we are being more productive through inhabiting two worlds at the same time. We are not. Instead, we move about in relative limbo: neither fully engaged in the here-and-now nor completely devoted to the matters that distracted us in the first place. Our slavishness to newness is debilitating. Our desire to mediate the world through the convergence of technology assumes we are able to successfully operate a dual existence when we typically do well to negotiate our way around oncoming individuals on the pavement. Where does this desire to augment our experiences in the city come from?

In Europe, the reconstruction of many post-war cities gave rise to significant masterplans and large-scale urban projects that sought to redress poor living conditions and provide improved civic relations (irrespective of what was actually implemented). Parallel to this development, wider societal optimism in the power of technology to help construct our futures was burgeoning. This technocratic impulse prompted a wave of architecture groups including Archigram, Archizoom and Haus-Rucker-Co amongst many others to conceive of new approaches to architecture and thus the creation of apparatus for mediating between the body and the built environment. The latter's *Environment Transformer* project of 1968 proposed, 'technoid helmets that expand horizons optically, abduct their wearers to a visual course of new perspectives on the urban surroundings' (Blomberg 2014, 32). Whilst the interest in speculative equipment continues to inspire elements of architecture education and research, this commitment to developing spatial paraphernalia to mediate and understand our environment also has a long history. Its value, as Geoff Manaugh explains, is that:

given the right instruments, humans gain access to and, more importantly, begin to interact with entire systems of objects and landscapes that were present all along but had otherwise been physically undetectable, camouflaged or hidden against an inhuman context or background. (2013, 27)

So where are we in the contemporary city and what does this mean for us? There appear to be two potential fields of influence at play here. Firstly, the fragmentation of urban space which, far from the order and legibility we may anticipate, has become complex and unintelligible (Jacobs 2002). This has led to a tendency to overlook the ordinary and commonplace but essential aspects of the urban landscape. Secondly, is the parallel movement of the growing reliance on data to assist our navigation and understanding of cities (Offenhuber and Ratti 2014). The capacity (if not always capability) of mobile devices to provide us with continuously updated and precise information about our surroundings can be very useful, especially for those unfamiliar with their context or seeking new knowledge on places. But there is a cost. By their very definition interfaces also sieve our relationship with cities, gently and surreptitiously nudging us toward particular locations based on an aggregated logic of data mining and stored personal preferences. More fundamental with regard to directly engaging with the city is that such devices are highly distracting. They reduce discovery and encounter because they present a mediated experience. This is an aspect most of us are fully aware of yet we find it hard to resist the seduction. The impact of this complicit coercion is totally immersive as our lives become saturated with 'representations' (Crawford 2015). What if we leave these versions and engage with the actual? Another question slides into view. How to make sense of any city, let alone at night where our reliance on the visual is at best diminished if not completely misleading? Way finding, that is locating and orientating oneself in the urban landscape, is an essential part of place making. However, our understanding of cities does not necessarily easily correlate to the formal descriptions offered by plans and cartography. Walter Benjamin describes this disorientation between the actual experience of the city and its many representations thus:

Now the city turns into a labyrinth for the newcomer. Streets that he had located far apart are yoked together by a corner like a pair of horses in a coachman's fist. The whole exciting sequence of topographical dummies that deceives him could only be shown by a film: the city is on its guard against him, masks itself, flees, intrigues, lures him to wander its circles to the point of exhaustion. But in the end, maps and plans are victorious: in bed at night, imagination juggles with real buildings, parks, and streets. (2005, 24)

More than half a century ago Kevin Lynch (1960) undertook pioneering research on how individuals perceive and navigate cities in order to better understand such phenomena. His seminal work, *The Image of the City*, explained that people understood their built environment via cognitive maps that facilitated their recall of information from the urban landscape using particular elements. Whether the contemporary city is as equally legible is highly questionable. Further complications arise when we transpose this mapping to the nocturnal city, which may resist familiarity and congruence. In fact we may experience alarm and discomfort due to our overreliance on the visual during the day, which may be significantly limited at night. Indeed, the threat of dark space is frequently perceived as the unnerving harbinger of the unseen, as Anthony Vidler discusses:

space is assumed to hide, in its darkest recesses and forgotten margins, all the objects of fear and phobia that have returned with such insistency to haunt the imaginations of those who have tried to stake out spaces to protect their health and happiness. (1992, 167)

Separating fear and darkness is no small task, especially given the depiction of cities at night, which, whether fictional or factualized, is often dramatic and threatening. It is here we enter what Bert de Munck (2004) defines as 'the prosthetic paradox.' This is a condition where the increased accumulation of surveillance technologies in our cities corresponds with greater feelings of anxiety and fear. Is it possible to embrace darkness positively? Certainly, rethinking our perception of it as not merely being the absence of light may be important. Minkowski (1933) and subsequently Caillois sought to encourage this perspective: 'There is something positive about it. While light space is eliminated by the materiality of objects, darkness is "filled," it touches the individual directly, envelops him, penetrates him, and even passes through him…' (Caillois 1987, 72). This kind of porosity between the body and the built environment is present in recent architectural theory:

> I confront the city with my body; my legs measure the length of the arcade and the width of the square; my gaze unconsciously projects my body onto the facade of the cathedral, where it roams over the mouldings and contours, sensing the size of recesses and projections; my body weight meets the mass of the cathedral door, and my hand grasps the door pull as I enter the dark void behind. I experience myself in the city, and the city exists through my embodied experience. The city and my body supplement and define each other. I dwell in the city and the city dwells in me. (Pallasmaa 2005, 40)

In this sense we are in flux with our surroundings and it becomes clear that materials temper our relationship with the environment both as constructions and physiologically.

Architecture is undoubtedly a spatial art, yet it may also be understood as a temporal one. The architect Peter Zumthor observes that our perception of atmosphere is intuitive, having evolved through an advanced emotional sensibility: 'Not every situation grants us time to make up our minds on whether or not we like something or whether indeed we might be better heading off in the opposite direction' (2006, 13). Such emotional sensibility is further sharpened in the nocturnal city when our eyes are less dependable as a means to make sense of what surrounds us. Moreover, the city itself transforms in character: simultaneously revealing and obscuring different elements as its architecture morphs and melds. For at night the entire city can become spolia for new monuments. It is these rich, otherworldly qualities of the everyday environment cast into shadow that stir 'the whole fauna of human fantasies,' which Louis Aragon identified 'drifts and luxuriates in the dimly lit zones of human activity, as though plaiting thick tresses of darkness' (1994, 13). This is our departure point for sensing the nocturnal city but also considering how we may relate to its broader surrounding landscape.

Threaded down along the river, a rich vein of **memento mori** *for the city. The fuzz of distant light bobbles along the water's surface. The Irk, like the night, has a history of uneven tempo, once renowned for its speed then later akin to a large slug such was its apparent inertia. Onward and across Angel Meadows, a subplot for the district, solemnly resists further development of the next instalment of Manchester's rejuvenation program. The turf here quietly bridling with the mass grave of industrial past, the interned some of who were overturned as poverty led to the digging up of cemetery soil for sale as fertilizer for nearby farmers. Looming ahead, the globular spaceship of the Co-operative headquarters nestles into the urban warp and weft around it. Rochdale Road, a discreet fissure between pallid gentrification and bodged cosmetic surgery of renewal, strikes ahead, forging away from the city centre: an echo chamber of recurrent hopes and scuffed dreams. Tonight is cold in the lungs, the air turning them to brittle chambers that with each inhalation feel as though they might shatter. Crisp footsteps and the plumes of hydrated air accompany my perambulations. Dull metal-grey mini-submarines, discharged of gas for their hysteria, litter the doorway of an old mill. The laughing and jostling shadow forms having long moved onto another urban cove. The ramparts of the city's innards pulp here, yielding to exigencies of conflicting needs and desires.*

Graphic equalizers of the Band on the Wall's headdress count out the pulse. Disconnected from the audio inputs of the city or the music venue itself when open, the ultimate silent disco. But the city is not still not without noise. The cacophony of drinkers, clubbers and taxis may be gone but the hum of distant traffic is still legible. Closer by a feline-eyed shadow leaps onto the wall of the Smithfield Gardens housing estate. Once another compost heap for humanity, the dispossessed deported to the outer suburbs, its replacement of orange-red maisonettes work on their own internal logic. Tib Street, the menagerie of birds and animals displayed along this bone of the city gone too. Dispensed between the stubbed side streets and poured onto Oldham Street. This road used to witness the parading of people in their Sunday best, consuming the stores' windows and eyeing up each other. Strict moral codes, ladies on one side, gentlemen on the other. Tonight though, the only attention coming my way is from a drained, rattling can, its energy-drink contents seemingly not giving up the ghost just yet.

Space Invaders score upon the walls around this district; ceramic-tiled street art of a latent network. Fire escapes hang above, the rebranding of the area two decades ago as the Northern Quarter testament to its fluidity for this is also the New York of remade and remodelled images of the cinema on a budget. Piccadilly Basin puddles ahead, the landscape opening up now. Former mills and warehouses stripped of their function and now accommodating the storage of city dreamers' and loft livers' bulk on either side. Strangely redundant in use unlike their inhabitants, the work-hard-play-hard mantra vibrates through the brick. The lazy S of Gateway House sleeks toward the way on. The railway station empty yet open, shuttered retailers and information matrix boards speaking to no one. In. Across. Down. Out. The taxi rank slowly rolls its cars around the circuit. Two drivers chatting to each other whilst elsewhere the solitary figures stationed behind steering wheels talk to Bluetoothed, faraway ghosts. The Star and Garter, a final ragged nail in the slick redevelopment plan – the indie disco at the end of the world – awaits its fate. Arrive here on a couple of occasions throughout the year at this hour and you will see be-quiffed individuals of all shapes, sizes, ages and ethnicities in homage to Steven Patrick Morrissey, one of the city's most famous sons, at the longstanding Smiths Tribute Night.

The Mayfield Depot looms large here, briefly ignited into being during the Manchester International Festival in 2013, embers of potential longer-term development quickly extinguished by local residents over concerns about noise pollution. We'll see. Curving round the back of Piccadilly Station, furtive glances from the guy in the car watching the tendrils of red-light activity flow through the surrounding back streets and behind. Industrial estates and apartment blocks, zipped together by Great Ancoats Street – a four-lane barrier that severs the city centre from its nearest northern living neighbourhoods. New

Islington, a partially developed area breathed some new life via Will Allsop's big handprint. The future is still yet to arrive as the school and other key buildings remain undeveloped yet. The Cardroom Estate's replacement via FAT as a Millennium Community has divided and displaced a tightly knit group but perhaps the most significant obstacle is perceptual, with newer settlers of students and young professionals alike all boltholing between dwelling and the city centre. The opportunities of the basin and canals somewhat compromised by the tired retail park offer that shoulders into the area. Store Street lures the feet back into the city centre. Stuffed under Station Approach again, the Warehouse Project: for 12 weeks the city is ours. Not tonight for the sanitized rave experience, its club thump and pump faded out months ago. Twisted Wheel to Club Lash to Homoelectric: the cavalcade of nights for the pleasure principle continues its lineage but the disco lights are dimming round here as hotels and apartments stomp into the picture.

Round the corner and across the street the railway viaduct undulates. Through one of the arched portals the whole mise en scène *of UMIST, Manchester's miniature Brasilia, is almost luminescent. The complex of buildings and multi-levelled access a real showstopper for the modernist, perhaps the city's ultimate essay in concrete and glass. Confidence rarely cast so bold within the inner ring road. A hairpin route the result of a narrow street and through the heady aromas and neon blur of Chinatown. This district of the city may be its one real claim to the 24/7 aspirations. Pause.*

I am now compressed in the wonderful push-pull of Library Walk. Perhaps the most dynamic open space in the city but not for much longer. Its nights are numbered, soon to become an impasse as the place is shielded from public feet and fettered with shiny, bulbous science-fiction adornments. This thing called progress lacerates the enchanting and favours the money. Derelict ideology requires the demolition of the cherished and savoured, all built on the shifting sands of finance. Booth Street cautions the legs past the police headquarters – nothing to see here officers. Then a dogleg across Deansgate and down towards the discordance of the Museum of Science and Industry and the excavated sets for Coronation Street. *Castlefield bowls out too soon to stack after stack of apartment blocks. Industrial heritage and its ruins crisscross around here, infrastructural behemoths of former success now speechless, corroding and beautiful. The origins of the city lie here, Mancunium, civic stones, the very bones of former settlements desecrated for the progress of the canal and railway, now reconstructed as heritage motifs for public acknowledgement. Eerie and vulnerable, the massiveness of the area and its artefacts is pliable and yields to the feet easily as archways and pillar frame new views and oddments of the past.*

Connecting:

Hinterlands of the body and the city

And I wander in this endless territory, through the distances
inside of me,
Crossing the territory inside, it wants to keep me in here.
What's behind – spiralling away unseen?

—LoneLady, *Silvering* (2014)

At the edge of the city, its artificial illumination begins to lose some of its hold against the firmament of night. Streetlight punctuations bend away from the built aggregation, chasing down roads to the next amber-white network. Out here, in the hinterlands of the city, the manufactured landscapes of industrial processes, production and distribution may be found, perhaps landlocked within larger swathes of agrarian territory. This is 'the unofficial countryside' that Richard Mabey mapped out during the early 1970s, bringing attention to the overlooked, crumbling and scrubby fringes of cities. Before him Richard Jefferies in the late nineteenth century published *Nature Near London*, which sought to bring a keen eye to the ragged edges and interstitial zones between the city and countryside. These places err around their own identity. Liminal zones of secondary and tertiary concerns for the city, abandoned buildings, lock-up garages, power sub-stations, gullies, fences, gravel paths ending abruptly – Keep Out, Danger, Trespassers Will Be Prosecuted – homemade testaments to ward off the unwelcome and unwanted. Time is a warrant here. Chance encounters are far more seldom than in the city but the isolation deepens the effect of any exposure. As such, ears are perpetual barometers for the shifting landscape, keenly pinpointing any sound distinct above the low faraway shush of the motorway. To explore the hinterlands of the nocturnal city is to rediscover and connect with the places intrinsic to the push and pull of the urban fabric albeit with its own distinctive character. They may have a proximity to our home but the experience can be as exotic as any far-flung destination on a bucket list.

Walking out of the city in the twenty-first century is not always a die-cut transition between the urban and the not-urban, as if being in and being out are liable to the city walls of centuries ago. A few years ago I walked around Detroit and the lack of distinction between in and out of the city there was incomparable to anywhere else I have been. As Jerry Herron accurately defined the situation, 'Detroit may be emptied out, then, but it is hardly over, nor will it be anytime soon, precisely because of the questions that this city/not raises' (2010, 78). The patchwork ecotones at the edge of cities resist easy classification, a situation even more opaque at night. For during nocturnal hours, these areas are the true black box of the city, holding its secrets, economies, demands and distribution networks together. Large, faceless blocks serviced by forklift trucks and their larger, articulated brethren. In the day, such distribution centres are also stark with tonal palettes of greens or blues gradated to blend with land or sky. At night, such clumsy camouflage is useless against the horizon, forming vast *2001: A Space Odyssey* monoliths of mystery and internal logistics. These Area 51 bases of consumerism occupy their sites as the result of maximum efficiency and logistics' triumph over space.

The semi-bucolic parts of the outer city receive a supernatural patina at night, as the roiling darkness surrounds them. Inverted scoops of light flood farmyards and adjacent land, cutting sharply between the oversaturated and unlit. Across the undulating arable landscape, these squat beacons map out a strange braille of grain, poultry, swine and bovine. For the urban nightwalker, such a terrain may be initially disconcerting as it only holds remnants of the familiar. As much as the city reaches its limits here, so does the body as it yields to the darkness palpably. Italo Calvino could well have been describing the hinterlands of the nocturnal city when he wrote, 'If you want to know how much darkness there is around you, you must sharpen your eyes, peering at the faint lights in the distance' (1997, 51). Insomuch as we are able to comprehend the holistic nature of the city when we are on the edge of it rather than within it, the anthropology of our own nocturnal body is also more apparent.

The history of human activity is intrinsic to our primary form of motion; it has been fundamental to our being present in the world and connected to the landscape. It seems evident that in our era of rapid technological development, the attentive and deeply situated relationship we may have with our urban landscape is easily lost. But being out on the edge of the city may require deeper concentration. The conservative rectitude that organizes the city loses its grip as the limits of its planning, zones and vested interests fade, its censorial technologies less effective. The ongoing flow between the land and the sky is perceptively *closer*. The distinctions that are clearer and sharper in the city at night are spongy here in the hinterlands. It becomes hard for the urban nightwalker to easily decipher this integration. As Tim Ingold has observed, 'the more one reads into the land, the more difficult it becomes to ascertain with any certainty where substances end and the medium begins' (2011, 119). Walking in these outer lands of the nocturnal city, the feet are welcomed by an array of soft, wet, crunchy, squelchy, inclined, swallowing surfaces and textures that are not present in the city's hard lines. The body is absorbed within the rhythms of these different materials and the movements they allow or prohibit. In this manner, 'the land itself no longer appears as an interface separating the two, but as a vaguely defined zone of admixture and intermingling' (119). Thus, the nightwalker also becomes an element of the medium between the land and the night sky. Plunged into a seemingly archaic and disturbing world, it is tempting to tug on the digital umbilical cord for reassurance but this would be to miss the pleasure of an immersive experience that is much scarcer and harder to locate in the city itself. Indeed the precipitous nature of being outside of the city at night can be daunting. The primeval qualities bristle on the skin as the unfamiliar arrives in a continuous line through the act of walking. Faith must be placed in the feet then.

Nocturnal peregrinations require a deep breath and a conscious untethering from digital handheld technology in order to enable us to engage intensely with the tangible. The urban-edge and its environs are alloyed to the weather and different levels of light in a way that is incomparable within the city. This is a time and place across which we should let go of ourselves. The landscape of the feet and mind are willingly in tandem, as they often need to give full attention to the ridges, furrows of earth and ideas presented to them. The urge to go out into the night and savour its restorative properties from negative daily intrusions chimes with Solnit's reasoning to go out walking, since it 'is one way of maintaining a bulwark against this erosion of the mind, the body, the landscape and the city, and every walker is on guard to protect the ineffable' (2000, 11). However, to disconnect is no straightforward task; in fact it is *work*. Our contemporary fear of missing out intertwined with immediate and nonstop social media represents the 'end of absence' (Harris 2014). However, we may wish to reconsider what we really give our attention to, as Zygmunt Bauman has suggested:

> Contrary to an impression made common in the modern era, procrastination is not a matter of sloth, indolence or lassitude; it is an active stance, an attempt to assume control over the sequence of events and make that sequence different from what it would be were one to stay docile and unresisting. (2000, 134)

From this perspective, therefore, walking at night may be understood to be a subtle act of resistance toward the limits of the day to day. Why should this matter? Intrinsic to a withdrawal from our environment is a decline in our first-hand awareness and knowledge of place and each other. Digital proxies are slippery. On the one hand they appear to inform us of everything we need to know; the sheer quantity of data can be beguiling. But, on the other hand, the quality of information is not necessarily rich, accurate or, most importantly, a substitute for direct experience. Conceived in this way, it is possible to understand first-hand encounter as relational rather than absolute. This correlates with anthropological work on vectors since they are inherently *motile* and point toward the enduring and fluctuating nature of relationships (Gatt 2013). This indeterminacy and fluidity is key to understanding our environment and our contingent roles within it and with each other. Rather than fixed and solid, the city and its edge zones at night may evolve into the 'terrain vague,' described by Lévesque as:

> an indeterminate space without precise boundaries… a place… outside the circuit of the productive structures of the city, an internal, uninhabited, unproductive and often dangerous island, simultaneously on the margins of the urban system and a fundamental part of the system… the counter image of the city, both in the sense of a critique and a clue for a possible way to go beyond. (2002)

Why venture into the metropolitan hinterlands? Walking in urban landscapes and their outer zones at night naturally draws our attention toward limits: the confines of the day, the parameters of regular journeys or the restrictions of routine. As Georg Simmel noted, the 'boundary is not a spatial fact with sociological consequences, but a sociological fact that forms itself spatially' (1997, 143). To go out walking into the night is a critical act counter to both perceived and concrete boundaries. Being on the edge of the city, the nightwalker is rewarded with an often-spectacular dual aspect of possibility. In the first instance, the city may be seen as the orange-white constellation it is at night, rolled out across the land – a dot-to-dot domain of connexion. Secondly, the body may be able to experience greater levels of darkness beyond the urban night.

True darkness is incredibly rare and hard to discover (or should that be recover) around most cities due to the different types of light pollution that stretch out of the city and reflect beyond its limits. The results of this upon the natural world have generally been disruptive if not downright disastrous in some locations. Disorientating wildlife, dispossessing animals from their habitat or decimating their behavioural patterns. The plight of tens of thousands of birds trapped in the 9/11 memorial, The Tribute in Light, in New York is a high-profile example of a situation caused by artificial lighting in cities replicated elsewhere around the globe (Talanova 2015). In response to this, alongside further environmental concerns, there has been growing determination to protect our night skies through official organizations and community groups. Attempts to reclaim the wonder of the galaxies and the highly affective chiaroscuro of moonlight have become a significant recent priority (Attlee 2011, Bogard 2013). However, for most of us the true dark sky is an aberration from the indolent haze that hugs our cities. Writing about their own experiences of forgotten spaces, Paul Farley and Michael Symmons Roberts explain the struggle of finding truly dark places:

In early twenty-first century England, such darkness is much harder to find. There are three kinds of light pollution: 'sky glow' is the aura visible above our urban areas, amplified by water droplets in the air and other particulate matter; 'glare' is the fixed and intense brightness created by golf driving ranges or distribution centres or rail maintenance gangs; 'light trespass' is the general leakage of artificial light from badly designed street lamps or security lamps. Light itself has become toxic. (2011, 233)

However, to use artificial lighting to simply enable night to function in a similar manner to day is also to tamper greatly with its distinctive characteristics. It is perverse. Schlör points toward the fundamental essence thus: '[Firstly,] the night tells one how the city really is, how "the whole" functions; and secondly, night, and only night, represents the presence of the past, the myth, in the city of the present' (2013, 242). It is this conjuring of memory, presence and attention that makes nightwalking such a deep and multi-sensory experience. The ability for the body to be fully encompassed in the night occurs in the liminal zones at the edge of the urban landscape. For it is here that the alien nature of how we live in cities becomes transparent. Like the zone in Tarkovsky's *Stalker*, these edgelands may reveal some of our true character, no longer obfuscated by the urban detritus that we accumulate. The hinterlands, therefore, are a slowly desilvering mirror to our own existence, showing us tantalizing glimpses and refractions of different ways of living and being. Although we may not experience complete darkness here, compared to the 'night' we have become accustomed to within the city, there is far less direct and diffuse light. An eeriness washes over the urban dweller, the heightened lack of visibility further exacerbated as the mind races, summoning forth all possible terrors swiftly from across each field and behind each hedgerow or tree. The wired hum of electricity above reminds us of the flimsy connections to the supposed *civitas*. It is here that we can vanquish the day's chores and constrictions readily.

There are a good number of reasons to do this. Pleasure. Release. Creativity. Thought. Peace. These positive aspects of being often combine when nightwalking, to enable – or should that be *afford* – us to break out of the 'non-stop inertia' (Southwood 2011) that dominates our lives. Macerated by the liquidity of capital and the 'multi-faceted, generalized flexibility' of the network society (Castells 2000, 296) we find ourselves stuck: embalmed in technology and sinking out of touch with the physical world. But all is not lost. To nightwalk is to be sluiced of this jelly and replenished by real options and decisions guided by intuition and environment. Ideas are free to roam around and wander out here. At the urban edge, the possibilities are far-reaching and seemingly limitless. Notions gathered within the nocturnal city may be reflected on, gently percolating their way around the synapses, breathing in and out: they become alive. Being out and about at night presents opportunities to attend not only to the world around but also to oneself closely. This may be understood as a process of *becoming* an ongoing claim for introspection, which can be difficult to achieve or even access during the day. As John Muir noted, 'I only went out for a walk, and finally concluded to stay out till sundown, for going, out, I found was really going in' (1979 [1938], 439). From my experience, the values of nightwalking mirror this sentiment but with greater currency for contemporary lives in a state of constant distraction. It is precisely by connecting to the edges of what is thinkable parallel to being amongst the liminal zones of the city that it is possible to truly go *in*. That is, to escape the day-to-day and be within the overlapping thresholds of identity, place and ideation. What can be so instrumental and invigorating about this process is the extraordinariness of the commonplace. To expand on this point, what I mean here is that we are usually so bound up in inconsequential, but at the time apparently urgent, and multiple matters of the everyday is that it is easy to ignore the importance of the ordinary. Robert Macfarlane describes the initial difficulty in accepting such a landscape as a place that requires its own special investigations:

> The notion of developing a relationship with this mixed-up, messed-up terrain did not occur to me. Disruptive of the picturesque, dismissive of the sublime, this was a landscape that required a literacy I didn't then possess: an aesthetic flexible enough to accommodate fly-tipping, dog shit, the night-glare of arc lights at the park-and-ride, and the *pock-pock-pock* of golf balls being struck up the driving range by architects and fund managers – as well as the yapping laugh of green woodpeckers through beech trees. (2015, 237)

Indeed, as he acknowledges, it can take a while until this

'literacy' is acquired, with time and proximity both being key elements to developing it. However, the pleasure of revelation, especially at night, within the overlooked adjacent lands of suburbia can be astonishing. As a result, when we do finally give our attention to it, it can be mesmerizing and rewarding – perhaps a sad sign of how disconnected we have become. Connecting back into the landscape at night, then, is obviously not a primarily visual exercise but one that concerns a combinative eidetic process drawn from all senses. In his discussion of this process, James Corner describes it as:

> a mental conception that may be picturable but may equally be acoustic, tactile, cognitive, or intuitive. Thus, unlike the purely retinal impression of pictures, eidetic images contain a broad range of ideas that lie at the core of human creativity. (1999, 153)

By contrast to Corner's discussion on the role of different drawing techniques in forming a dialogue with mental images, here we are talking about the deliberate looseness and multi-sensory experience of linking with the peripheral urban landscape as conducive to offering prompts and symbols to help shape our ideas. To develop this a bit further, the very absence of both visibility and purposefulness is the *matter* of such exploration and imagination.

This is the overlap of our own and the nocturnal city's limits. There is a distinct timbre to the outskirts of cities, the not quite urban which blends effectively with the not quite dark. This entanglement is not simply physiological but also psychological. At the edge of what we might call nature and its abutment with the (sub/extra/post-) urban is a mindset. It stirs strongly from within. It recalls our primeval origins and connection to the land beneath our feet. Half-forgotten words and phrases, dialects for disappearing worlds leach from the earth. Our need for enclosure and control – of the land, our roles, our minds, our behaviour – is all laid out here. Subjugation to the powers that be – a manufactured landscape for maximum yield. Attention and creativity are no better treated, technological and social lock-in lead to depleted and undernourished ideas. We have sold our rights without ever reading the small print. The terms and conditions of the city lose their power here, a world beyond which always hovers at its edge: it 'broods and waits' (Papadimitriou 2012). Yet somehow it never *arrives* either. It is simultaneously elegiac and uplifting. This is the promise and the premise of being in the urban hinterlands at night. The process of becoming is never fulfilled but ongoing; a deep and tangled relationship between identity and place will be more in flux and open to interpretation than in the city. The difference is in the speed. In the city, the rapidity of change is explicit, even in the slow time, glow time of night. But out at the nocturnal city's perimeter, the transformation is more fundamental. Both are essential for they are conjoined, inseparable in their being. To tap into this landscape at night is to conjure up those previous pilgrimages and protests of the night that echo throughout history. It is easy to imagine the shady worlds of miscreants, sneaks and transgressors out here, moving across the dimly lit landscape toward their goal. In the twenty-first century, these outer regions of the city are at odds with what we understand to be important to our always-on, always-connected, networked lives. Instead they may appear disconnected, hitherto abandoned and outside of the pulse and demands of the capitalist dome. This indeed may be their core value. To go beyond, literally outside of the construct, is to see its wondrous attributes and its flaws. Stepping out of the burnished and illuminated city at night and venturing to its edges is to recalibrate your relationship with it. This is both physical and in the psyche. The mindscape is less piqued and freer to roam around, unfettered by the multiple technological and material boundaries that accumulate in the city to protect its interests.

Profiteering in the hinterlands of the nocturnal city is either brazen or buried deep. The sequestering of land for multi-national corporations and regional companies to distribute goods and services lays claim to tracts of the landscape that bring with them the accoutrements of business, played out in a self-referential game to consolidate ownership. Elsewhere, the signs are far less obvious. Missing equipment, liberated goods and illegal substances trade out of blacked-out 4x4 vehicles and high performance cars - a delaminated gentry hovering around the margins of the nocturnal landscape. The poachers here are of your time and capital, recirculating the products of systemic downfall and taking us away from what really matters and deserves our attention. Outliers, interlopers and small-time operators dream big as they look back toward the nocturnal city. Wandering and wondering in the liminal froth of the urban landscape is a continual dialogue between the edge of the city at your feet and the imagined city always just around the corner, slightly out of view in your thoughts.

Some of my early formative experiences of night and landscape were near the soft estate that stretched alongside the top of the M60 motorway (though it was yet to be known as such until 2000 and at the time was part of the M62). Underpasses and steep verges provided beguiling geometry and darkness enlivened by the loud grumbling of traffic overhead. At night, the interspersed noise of heavy-goods vehicles and cars amongst eerie quiet and barely audible wildlife, both washed together by the rustling of leaves and branches in the wind. Within these areas of hinterland there was dark matter: unfathomable, unnameable and unknown. From a child's perspective it seemed to be something alien. Powder-coated leaves, dusted by the road; wildness abruptly halted as the bitumen shouldered hard against it; and, of course, no lighting for you are not supposed to be there. As an adult revisiting these sites there are obvious changes, the weird and otherworldly feel that was essentially the lack of visibility mixed with a vivid and less rational imagination is significantly lessened. By contrast, the strange dislocation of being in these places – at once in tandem yet also off-kilter with the world – is extremely poignant. Being closely allied with the edge of the nocturnal city here – feeling the vibrations of its vehicular comings and goings, yet being visibly detached and almost marooned in an apparently subterranean woodland – is a very particular experience. It enables the peripheries of the mind to be explored in a way that is difficult to achieve in the city centre. The solitude is visceral. Beyond any line of vision, the thrum of unseen wheels filters through the trees to provide a consistent soundtrack: comforting and reminding of the wider world. Time spent in places such as this is dense and slow-moving, the night sky pivoting around imperceptibly with birds announcing the changing state and oncoming of sunrise. This helps us reconnect and rebalance our relationship with the environment. In *What Time Is This Place*, Kevin Lynch noted the destructive effects of being out of synch with it:

> Our environment subjects us to potent rhythms, many now man-created, many out of phase or experienced haphazardly. We fly from time zone to zone. Our attention ebbs in protracted meetings; after lunch we long for the nap we cannot take. We resist spring fever and fail to act energetically when we are most alert. We may be wakeful at bedtime and dull in the morning. As the seasons change, we carry out the same schedule in daylight and darkness. Our health depends on an integrated internal time structure, well joined to external periodicities. Perhaps we could begin to read the time structure proper to our own bodies. (1972, 119)

Nightwalking, therefore, may be understood as one way in which the body can settle into a more harmonious relationship with the environment. It enables the wakeful to enjoy and take full advantage of what is often viewed as unproductive time. It also connects us back with who we are and *when*, offering a contemplative place and time to reflect and allow biological predispositions to take centre-stage. Not only does walking at night free the mind but it also presents new visceral experiences. Unlike in the city, out here the feet leave marks across the land: demonstrable impressions pushed into the mud and soil, monstrous in scale compared to other creatures' foils that trace and weave across it. Human scent is far clumsier too, stretching out into the darkness ahead of the body and with it the briefest flash of vulpine eyes and the sound of disturbed undergrowth. Backing away from the motorway and the tenebrous and untamed landscape brusquely meets domesticated gardens, fences, hedges and occasional flashpoints of home-security lights with poorly orientated sensors. In a moment, the nonchalant paws of a cat moving across a rear lawn turn the whole scene ablaze with light, flooding the garden and jabbing out in slices through the fence. And in this instant, I too am transformed from being an amorphous, slowly travelling mass blurred into the surroundings to become a stark, sharp-edged human, separate from the environment. Further along the ground joins in the formality and gravel greets the feet with crunchy kisses until the forlorn figure of a lamppost reaches out with its rays down a ginnel to resurface me at street level.

Back in the suburban logic of semi-coiffed nature, driveways and double-glazed dwellings, the homes are oddly neutral to the nightwalker despite their variations on a theme. Perhaps the sheer banality induces a mental torpor that, akin to a flywheel, releases the feet to an unprecedented speed, pounding out the tarmac paths and concrete pavement until the flight from suburban fugue is complete. Exit velocity bursts through the ozone of tasteful repetition, with personalized accents, and now the nocturnal city's centripetal pull can be felt again. Drawn toward the haze of murky orange-grey tones, the solid silhouettes against the sky with luminous pixels, and the increasing lofi noise of urbanism building up and onwards to the centre of the city and its intoxicating pathologies.

Infrastructural heaven. The orbital motorway flies overhead and the city is framed by the Barton High Level Bridge. Less dominant in the skyline but more arresting is the Barton Swing Aqueduct, the only one of its kind in the world, which carries the Bridgewater Canal over the Manchester Ship Canal. Behold another cathedral to consumerism, the Trafford Centre. Victor Gruen's principles set out in a mash-up of Rococo and Late Baroque styles with some hefty chunks of Art Deco and Egyptian Revival stirred into the architectural hotpot. It draws denizens from all over the North West and beyond to its lurid display and free parking. This is the spectacle of society: total immersion into the leisure-industrial multiplex of retail and opulence. It is truly bewildering. The area's former industrial past is changing; the light-rail transit no longer shunts along the tracks, warehouses swapping footprints with office parks.

Cornflakes. The Kellogg's factory wafts its cloud of baked cereal smells across the district. Bearing right towards Stretford and past the unblinking eyes of the gold plastic Alsatian, always in attendance on its balcony regardless of time or season. Around the park and straight over Chester Road, one the city's main arteries but devoid of traffic now save for the distant fading rear lights stretching away. The former cinema, listed but inert, an Art Deco bulwark for regeneration and revisionist plans yet to be implemented. Sidling over the hump of the canal and tramlines and downwards. Longford Park brings with it the muted sounds of the suburbs, more of South Manchester neatly arranged in view and temper. It is calm and collected here, the leafy and clean streets of the M21 postcode giving no clue to its infamy as the most burgled area in the country. A dotted line traversed between back-to-back terraced houses and then over gravestones to the woods beyond. From bitumen to cobbles, transition felt keenly underfoot. Displaced stone teeth of the path, a gappy grimaced rupture as one adjacent tree is unwilling to accept the aphercotropic fate befallen to so many. The stones yield to mud and narrower paths disperse into the after-gloam. Decision time. Left and the path threads along the edge of a field, the fencing has seen better times and the drooping slope elevates the view across. Over the horse stile and now the river bulges into view. Down the steep bank to the water and along, treading carefully on a mixture of mud, turf and semi-concealed rocks.

The pylon filigree makes poor company for its silver-birch brethren in the dim, clouded moonlight as the molten ebony of the Mersey River smears past below. Pushing up the riverbank, past the flood line of winter swelling, and across the bridge toward the scanty woods. A tent in the trees seems to be losing its tautness against the weather. Somewhere in the undergrowth, a small fox stirs and then skits across the path away from the crunch of boots and human scent. Drizzle brings with it an ocular sharpening as the edges of flora and the longer grasses suddenly lean into view, the murky assemblage instantly composed like decoupage. Onward towards Wythenshawe, that bastion of Garden City displacement where the pitch shifter of the landscape alters from deadened calm and occasional rustling to an altogether more eerie quiet.

Emerging from the jaundiced concrete flyover that arcs a man-made swathe and announces the end of nature, the rain increases in quantity and quality. No longer the spritz of a light shower but aqua javelins ready to skewer anything set before them to the earth. Sodden and cowed, limbs trudge powered by steamed breath toward the suburban fringe ahead. Rheumy homes line the perspective on either side as rivulets gather and grow on every surface. A car sheens its way around the corner, lights off then headlights all ablaze as its exit velocity from the estate increases exponentially into the murk beyond. It's quiet here, save for the rain. Satellite lives flicker lonely blues and greens behind glass portals and the distant smeared sounds of cars over the rooftops brum and fade away. Several turns later and the edge of Wythenshawe Park cascades away either side of me. The sentry of trees are filtered through and the vast carpet of the park rolls out, a luxurious deep-pile affair, feet sinking into the soft surface, bedecked with curvaceous mirrors where the land lies low and is saturated. The puddles stare back, reflecting the clouds overhead and a damp and dishevelled silhouette. The ground offers poor resistance to leather and rubber rhythms, instead pulling each footstep further into the quagmire and pooling rainwater with each depression.

Creature stirrings and feathered fluttering nuzzle the air alongside the community farm, the slightest murmur amplified in the viscosity of the shadows. Far from foreboding but unquestionably supernatural in tone having left behind the manmade landscape for something more serene and softer in texture, the verdant silhouettes crinkle in the background air. Onwards to the light-industrial estates of Benchill, boxed and coxed to order. Augé would have a field day here as non-place and non-time conspire to a landscape replicable anywhere around a city's edge. Blank sheds and van bulkheads secure their space. Fences, gates, sentry points and vehicle barriers hold the outside world back from the logistics of loading bays, turning circles and other intriguing surface marks. Apart from the distant squawk of a security radio, the syncopated rumble of traffic along the M56 provides the musique concrète *of this segment of the journey. The road dips and rises over motorway and railway but then steadily climbs, converging with the dotted lines of blinking aircraft toward the airport. Following the slow curlicular path into the tunnels underneath the runways, the various jet propulsions of rubber against asphalt launch hundreds into the navy-black beyond or reverse engineer the process bringing them home. Beyond, the luxury plains of Cheshire roll out toward the horizon; they shall be explored on a longer and drier outing.*

Thinking:

The pathology of the urban night

The sun lies exhausted, endless amber streaks past,
A distant heart – hung with loss, nameless black beyond the
glass.

— The Obsession, Exit Wounds (2003)

The attitudes that beset so many of us regarding the night are borne of long-held beliefs, the origin of which demonstrates how little we still know and understand about the nighttime. Rooted in medieval practices, superstitions and fears, the contemporary hex of the city and its environs is most likely to be a very visceral but unlucky encounter with a pack of sport-branded classics rather than the invasive and shadowy hauntings of imaginary spectres and grisly halflings. This is the very essence of our worries, some of our deepest and, literally, darkest thoughts. What *is* out there? Those noises, so readily dismissed in daylight hours suddenly take on an entirely different timbre. The easily understood and rationalized becomes jumbled and disorientating as the crepuscular fabric of night stitches us in space and time to something altogether more worrisome.

Going out into the night can require explanation, to others and perhaps in a more complicated way to oneself. This extends the justification of time we are so familiar with during the day. Perhaps the single most profitable turn of late capitalism was the leisure market. By splicing and dicing 'free' time into consumer-orientated parcels, the desire to spend both time and money is a way of remaining tethered to the construct that dictates the daytime and work. Simply irresistible and so pervasive it is sometimes difficult to even recognize when we are resting, the mind saturated through endless signals of commoditization. This behaviour is so endemic to the twenty-first century that we find it incredibly difficult to turn off, tune out and drop away. Whether this will have long-term implications for us physiologically remains to be seen but the evidence appears to be building. Our attention is ravaged in pursuit of endless and mindless *plaisir*. We need to break out and go beyond the pleasure dome. Casting asunder wave after wave of information, we surf the web whilst rarely questioning whether we wanted to be in the digital deluge in the first place. Younger generations are deeply enmeshed in the matrix to the extent that it is invisible to them and *is* their reality. They are locked into what Mark Fisher (2009) has defined as 'reflexive impotence' whereby knowing how bad things are renders them unable to respond and ultimately becomes self-fulfilling prophecy. An empty, global-sized joke that will be desperately unfunny once the hysteria subsides and we stare into the cluttered and consolidated spaces of late capitalism. Perhaps one possible way out may be found in the derelict and desolate.

Urban areas are pathological. The nocturnal dowser can summon these neuroses effortlessly; such is the power upon our subconscious of nightfall and the city's shadows. Our fears reside in there. Of course, contemporary depictions do little to assure us that the nighttime city isn't full of the terminally sad, bad or mad. News bulletins and headlines aggregate and skew the 'night,' further exacerbating its otherworldliness. The crepuscular fabric of cities have featured in many film narratives, even providing the dominant character in films such as Mike Leigh's *Naked* (1993), Stephen Frears' *Dirty Pretty Things* (2002) or the fragmented interface between the CCTV scanscape and niches of impropriety depicted in Andrea Arnold's *Red Road* (2006). The sclerotic set of conditions presented in each of these three films depicts a raw portrait of the world, bleak urban landscapes of rejection, exploitation and violence. Spatial interstices and latent networks, away from primary routes of circulation, enable the protagonists in the films to occupy niches within the city, but only ever as fragmentary and temporary habitats since with negligible comfort they are always surreptitiously urged onwards. A common theme across the three works is the subsumption of the characters by their immediate surroundings that serves to intensify the direct correlation between the materiality of the city and themselves; the effects of weathering and neglect present in both the built fabric and the psyche. Social and physical deterioration as illustrated in this way contributes to the sometimes disorientating and disturbing effects of hauntology within urban places. The magnification and condensation of seemingly everyday experiences within fictional narratives, whether filmic, musical or written, cannot but feed our imagination. Shabby and shadowy carbuncular pockets of the city are brought vividly to mind as we recall the drama of such stories unfolding before us, a phantom overlay onto real place.

Nor do we have to *see* such events for them to resonate deeply within us. The ghosts of the city reverberate as industrial murmurs and metallic beats throughout LoneLady's most recent and sublime album, *Hinterland*. Inspired by her home city of Manchester, she constructs a post-industrial landscape of the mind wherein ideas have been ravaged by decay and decomposition, exposure to the elements and neglect. Yet, within these processes there is revitalization and replenishment. It is the very sense of abandonment and dereliction that enables explorations of the mental ruins and imperative to return to them repeatedly. There is recuperation within the broken and composition within the fragments. This is essential listening for the collapsing dreams of the twenty-first-century city. The cranking, motorik rhythms echo around as her voice maps out the landscape's niches and wastelands. The craving for sanctuary and the need to find oneself through exploration of the liminal zones of the post-industrial city is woven through the fabric of the sounds, textures and tenderness of her songs. This is a love letter to a disappearing landscape.

In a similar manner, the protagonist in Geoff Nicholson's *Bleeding London* is desperate to connect to the streets of the city through walking in order to access a deeper psyche. The character's methodical and unnerving practice of traversing each street in the city then deleting its corresponding entry in the London A–Z is bent upon an intuition that is simultaneously deranged and systematic in terms of his comprehension of and relationship to the urban landscape. Indeed, as he walks the streets he senses a powerful resonance that is beyond nostalgia:

'perhaps something behind history, behind events and personalities; mythic forms, archetypes, the old, old stories, something older than this city, something that is inherent in the very idea of the city' (1997, 194). In this situation, the city and the walker are one, a mindset steadily erasing abstract knowledge through direct experience.

All of these artistic statements by definition are affective and provocative. Real-world encounters and factual accounts can be equally influential to the memory and déjà vu sensation, which both imprint on later experiences of place. For several years in the mid to late nineties I worked as a freelance crime-scene surveyor. Forget the glossy Crime Scene Investigation sheen of televisual drama and action movies. The assignments I worked on were on sites of trauma within the city, largely but not exclusively nondescript interiors and domestic settings. This work took me to some of the most deprived and grim wards in the Greater Manchester region. Unthinkable acts by normal people, sometimes premeditated but often not. These were spaces subject to the full spectrum of violence and abuse. Without question, having witnessed the after burn of criminal actions, my perception of the city was deeply altered. This was not some remote dangerous land but within close proximity to where I resided at the time. Channelled potently through the media, it is small wonder that we are ossifying the 'fortress city' Mike Davis compellingly described in *City of Quartz* (1990). Designated, delineated and dedicated versus repellent, repulsive and regressive: the city in conflict with its own populace. Physical measures adorn boundaries and surfaces – metallic teeth to ward away the very flesh most in need of respite and recuperation. Meanwhile, the emolliated and dispossessed swell in number and voluntary organizations and charities desperately seek to provide necessary succour for them: increased and muted collateral from the banking bailout is seen but not heard.

In *The London Adventure, or the Art of Wandering*, Arthur

Machen posits: 'What about the tale of a man who "lost his way"; who became so entangled in some maze of imagination and speculation that the common, material ways of the world became of no significance to him?' (1924, 141). Although the work's wandering nature is reflective of Machen's own digressive urban walking, it is difficult to imagine being so completely ambivalent about the context of the city in the present time, especially at night. Indeed, part of the anxiety, charm and thrill (they are seldom isolated) of the nocturnal city is the not-knowing of what lies ahead, around a corner or in a shadow. So whilst it is tempting to think that all-consuming thoughts levitate the night-walker above ground, apprehension and awareness of urban pathologies continually ensure a degree of tethering to context, no matter how threadbare. Even in the twenty-first century, negative associations with darkness continue to pervade Western ideology. Darkness itself, meanwhile, is being obliterated. Literally squeezed out of the modern city through 'nocturnal-ization,' darkness has been 'transformed from primordial presence to a more manageable aspect of life' (Koslofsky 2011, 278).

This shift has not just been the preserve of organizational strategies and operational tactics to nullify the nocturnal city. It has also existed within artistic statements. Such fervour perhaps reached its zenith in Italian Futurist Marinetti's manifesto of 1909, with the proclamation that we should aim to 'kill the moonlight' in the onward surge towards a dynamic future of technological advancement. This is not an idea that has left us, as Williams explains:

> Because of its transgressive meanings and societally harmful uses, darkness threatens to deterritorialize the rationalizing order of society... when it obscures, obstructs, or otherwise hinders the deployment of the strategies, techniques, and technologies. (2008, 518)

As we have already learnt, in earlier periods of history darkness was understood to rise, the air palpably thicker with evil, ready to suffuse anything and anyone in its roil. Of course, the multifarious nature of events that beset mankind as daylight disappeared were also symptomatic rather than necessarily and directly caused by the night. Poor visibility, temperature drops, cover for miscreants to hide etc. The ultimate environment for sneaks of all kind. In *The Culture of Cities*, Lewis Mumford was keen to ascribe the unsettling and detrimental nature of being in the urban landscape:

> Living thus, year in and year out at second hand, remote from the nature that is outside them and no less remote from the nature within, handicapped as lovers and as parents by the routine of the metropolis and the constant spectre of insecurity and death that hovers over its bold towers and shadowed streets living thus the mass of inhabitants remain in a state bordering on the pathological. They become victims of phantasms, fears, obsessions, which bind them to ancestral patterns of behaviour. (1938, 258)

Even if the inhabitants of the city no longer need saving from themselves, then it is still easy to understand the considerable array of interventions that protect us from it. The preoccupation with *managing* urban space by definition constricts the sensual world; limiting the body's experience of pungent smells, rough textures and discordant sounds which spatial envelopes further shield from us. Given that so much of our interaction with each other in the daytime is predicated on the visual, the denial of this at night both optically (how our eyes work) and practically (there are typically not as many people around), we have to find new ways of connecting with and discovering our environment. Many aspects of the city that seem preordained during the day are open to interpretation at night – we become our own cartographers, forging maps from fused and complex sensory experiences rebalanced from daylight's prejudices. Richard Sennett goes so far as to argue that urban space has largely become 'a mere function of motion,' engendering a 'tactile sterility' which in turn leads to a pacifying of the body (1994, 15). He contends that the imperative to minimize disruption and distraction for pedestrians and drivers – to keep them focused on shopping, working and playing in *preferred* ways – means that movement is typified by rapid transit without arousal. In addition, the alluring qualities that drew our attention to the urban night throughout history are rapidly becoming an endangered species, caged and commoditized in commercial situations. Yet there still remains plenty of opportunity to explore the 'space' within cities, which, after all, is not a void, a neutral container or passive background for things to happen. On the contrary, it is a living entity in its own right. Sanford Kwinter describes space as 'a participant, an unstable and unpredictable process that both harvest and produces reality on the run' (2010, 74). Understood in this way, the structures of daytime can quickly break down at night, especially since our visual cognition attenuates and we may place greater reliability on the aural, olfactory and tactile, perhaps also the gustatory. Furthermore, the impact of materiality upon the sensory experience of walking becomes heightened and nuanced as place impresses itself on the pedestrian body and vice versa. Being present and directly experiencing through the spatial practice of walking is essential to uncovering a different understanding of our built environment that contradicts such manufactured smoothness. Considered in this manner, walking at night may be understood as an inscriptive practice, enriched with the potentialities that Bergson describes:

There do not exist things made, but only things in the making, not states that remain fixed, but only states in the process of change. Rest is never anything but apparent, or rather, relative. The consciousness we have of our own person in its continual flowing, introduces us to the interior of a reality on whose model we must imagine the others. (2012 [1913], 188)

The timorous and tentative paths we weave across our urban landscapes at night, unless locked in the spatial parley of overconsumption, reflect our uncertainty and belie our primeval origins. Being unsure of ourselves and, indeed, our unreliable relationship with the aphotic realm amplifies our nerves and the imagination folds in on itself at the potential maelstrom of the weird and wonderful, but most crucially, *unknown*. The typically nurturing interiors of buildings at nightfall lose their force field at the threshold, whether doorway or trapezoid of light surgically splicing the shaded world. Abstract sculptures of light restrain bins, doorways and shutters in their bondage. Furtive scratching in the surrounding gloom albeit for the catwalk saunter of a fox, long since acclimatized to the urban landscape. Overhead the blinking red eyes of an airplane arc outward and into the global convex airspace beyond.

But there is great disorder under heaven: fear, desolation, anxiety and the collapse of the modernist dream. Behold the twenty-first century city, in all its shimmering wonder and testament to capitalist accumulation. The role of the city from economic powerhouse and political machine through millennia of commerce and, more latterly, consumerism, has changed. Furthermore, the flattening of building façades facilitated by new technologies in the late nineteenth and early twentieth centuries have ensured that the membrane between inside and outside, whilst enticingly thinner than ever, is very real with less and less doorways, crevices, nooks and niches for shelter. Isolative urbanism at its finest. The shift of the city from being an arena of spectacle to a backdrop devoid of content is acute at night. Or so it seems. However, it is exactly in these unkempt, overlooked urban tributaries where nothing appears to be going on, i.e.

consumed, that the real *magick* resides. The nocturnal city is an adroit and dexterous dealer, for these places are reshuffled and laid out in different combinations depending on weather, season and regeneration. And, of course, not least: us. Cities can offer the celebration and resonation of small cycles of life, the freedom of movement, the joy of night and the personal. Why do this? The libations of the night are far from the backstreet dens of iniquity or those brash, magnificent temples to hedonism that pull together the corners of a street or animate a thoroughfare. No, this is a potion for all the senses to draught in carefully and slowly. Like molten wax the night air permeates the body, its pores and veins so that the boundary between human and environment blurs in the exchange of warm breath and cool intake. This is akin to swimming underwater and, similarly takes a bit of getting used to, but develops over time. That initial plunge into the unknown, the sensation of being underwater, the mild panic I felt as a child as water went up my nose, in my ears and blurred my eyes is reborn in a milder fashion the first time I step out into the night. It resurfaces every time I walk somewhere new, and sometimes recurs in places of familiarity. The heightening of the senses coupled with the deceleration of movement as the expanse of the city at night unfurls in every direction. The cold air numbs my ears whilst jabbing at my nostrils and my eyes water at this gentle facial pugilism. Meanwhile the initial stiffening of limbs and joints gradually gives way as the body regulates itself within the environs. The nyctophobia that blankets the subconscious at night, forestalls the imagination. To overcome this restriction is to embrace possibility, beauty and the grotesque. For this is the second city: out there, with its own landscape, population and movements. In this alternative world of shadows and nocturnal promise, the stirring and blurring of former times is palpable.

The hauntology, the combinative experience of past, present and ghost futures that never were, of walking through cities is immediate. Iain Sinclair is perhaps the best-known proponent of this activity, infiltrating the urban membrane and opening its pores for circumspection and revelation. At night such hauntology is seemingly beckoned forth so much more potently. Perhaps the intoxication of our fear of the unknown, suitably piqued in nocturnal hours, sharpens the sensitivity to, and further multiplies the abundance of the spirits held in their urban sarcophagus during the daylight hours. And out they are spewed from the shadows. The phantasmagoria of yesterday's planners, architects, city leaders, financiers and civic society cast all around. The facades tangibly ripple as the never quite dark transforms the sober and laconic and the misshapen and punch-drunk edifices alike. As they meld and wobble with each footstep, the city moves around the nightwalker – its sublime liquidity heavy and thick. When the surfaces of the city have been frosted, a muter, talcum landscape softens each viewpoint. When it has rained they glisten, the nightwalker embalmed in the vast amber onyx. Of course, when it is raining the motion is informed by the rivulets, gullies, drips and splashes of the shedding faces of the city. Edges may be clung to by way of shelter and here the nightwalker occupies a nichescape, veritable boltholes between which she or he can pause depending on the downpour and the distance. When considering *when* these places are, the ebb and flow of the diurnal pattern not only changes how and why we might access the nighttime but also the duration of the outing. Not for everyone a long, cold, perhaps even wet, nightwalk. Nor need it be. The wonderful atmosphere may be explored within different timeframes, variable distances and across a range of thresholds between dusk and dawn. Each episode is remarkable for its uniqueness but cumulatively the experience builds into quite a different composite. Familiarity is estranged even in those locations and traces closest in proximity to everyday routine. For here the habitus is disrupted. Gentle fingers fettle their way into the urban tissue, drawing the body into the night. Snout out, ears pricked back, the ecosystem welcomes another creature in the form of the nightwalker, an ambulatory, urban shadow roving across the landscape. The geometry of the city has shifted. Lights punch-holed into mass, oversensitive and poorly installed security lighting striking out as it detects nocturnal movement of some kind, hazy streetlights fuzz the sky and the faraway red pinpoints of towers and construction cranes as they impotently poke the night. The comparative lack of transport, especially cars, summons the ultimate refuting statement of the failed autoerotic utopia of the twentieth century we drove towards. Heathcote Williams' *Autogeddon* pile-up instead, inert and distributed, literally parked for *now* (1991).

Composting cities and the need to enable things to fail, perish and be redeveloped does not dovetail with unrestrained logics of late capitalism. Instead, empty sites that could support non-permanent, creative and social uses are simply bordered off, surgically removed from existence by perimeter fences, surveil-lance technology and the warnings of 24-hour call-and-response. Consequently, the most frequent re-use and temporary occupation of urban spaces is as open-air car parks. This unimag-inative and quick-fix intervention – often little more than a machine, some draconian threats wrought on signs and, sometimes, perimeter fencing – furthers our detachment from the city. It reinforces the notion that everything is to be consumed and space has a price. But what is the actual cost? One of the most difficult problems in trying to unravel this sort of development is being able to identify values beyond direct economic ones. Health, wellbeing, culture, nature, social relations are *essential* to us. Yet they are so often overlooked. Attempts to ascribe monetary value to these aspects have struggled to gain traction so far as the pervasive rapidity of the market is always able to twist and turn faster in response to any claims made against it.

If such spaces are out of bounds legally, the appropriation and illicit claims made upon them remain part of an ongoing tragicomedy rather than Jane Jacobs' gentle ballet of the street (1961). As for officially sanctioned strips of the city: the pavement and the pedestrian are coerced in the daytime, bonded within a double helix of restriction and entitlement, motion channelled, smoothed and conditioned. But at night, the urban landscape's delineation is smeared. Lines are dotted rather than forgone conclusions, the possibilities for smudging their bold and italicized strokes lies here. Walking at night repositions boundaries, inner and outer, renegotiating and rerouting them, a new layer of script swiftly erased with the sun.

Strangeways here we come. But first: the cathedral. Gothic Perpendicular upgraded from parish church and hewn from the stone of nearby Collyhurst. Beneath my feet, the nearby Victorian Arches – the prize in the urban explorer's eyes – tricky to access these days, encumbered by the river, the infrastructure and the resolute locking down of (no) entry points. Feel that? The gravitational field has been breached once again as the centripetal force of the inner ring road is crossed. Back against the M.E.N or "whateveritscallednow" arena, the city's mouth gapes open at this point. Boddington's brewery, an empty bootprint on the land, it's last days marked out with sanitized raves to the industrial totem pole, even its famous chimney subsequently demolished. Drawn out along Great Ducie Street and behold: the epic asterisk plan of brick. HMP Manchester will always be Strangeways to me, in the same way that for some Manchester Airport will always be Ringway, the rebranding and replaced signage never able to fully scrub the mind's palimpsest as ghost letters cling to their former sanctuary, the typescript stencilled in dirt. The streets either side of the prison are phantom escalators, feet unable to resist the upward heave of the compound's heft. A lone figure now set against a huge brick wall, multiple eyes of the surveillance cameras blankly looking back at me but unable to return any expression. My shadow grows and shrinks against the brick canvas in rhyme with the streetlights.

Upward and upward then plateau of light-industrial units, unspecified works and wholesalers that interlace with empty plots, restaurants and drinking dens until the froth of Cheetham Hill Road strikes across my path. This stretch of the city is an ongoing project of Non-Plan with its continual transformation: revisions and redactions of occupation and use. The incline underfoot steadily builds to Manchester Fort's circling of retail sheds. Wheelless and corralled, they lie in wait to engulf inner suburbaneers swashbuckling with bargain-hunters for discounted goods. Identikit and impoverished, replicable and regurgitated, these spaces continue to roll out around the UK: a terrible in-joke of architecture's footnotes in the great book of commercial development. Escape is at hand. Delving into the suburban fugue of Cheetham Hill, its architectural melodies changing as my feet trot down toward Higher Broughton. But the phrasing and composition of housing is imbibed with the long-established reshuffle of the recently settled. This is a rich and diverse swathe of the city. Scents and unknown dialects chatter and waft from homes, sensorial smorgasbord. The topography in this district is deep and dramatic, tumbling down toward the River Irwell, the streets are alive with plump plumes of urban life, piped ambition and dole(ful) dreaming.

No waterways tonight. Moving back into the amber glow of street lamps and more suburban ploy lies ahead. The recognizable rhythms of housing around here allow the mind to wander freely, hopping between ideas without obstacle. Half an hour of slow walking takes place. Along with it, the accompanying process of sketching out new directions and maps for previously under-nurtured concepts and projects. These thoughts need more space. What better than six-hundred acres of municipal park? The city's greatest green lung, Heaton Park usually has its paths locked and gated but tonight this one isn't. A few minutes pass by and the rolling surf of landscape all around me is overwhelming. Whatever you desire in your time out of the city it is here, from pitch 'n' putt to tracksuit and strut; boating lake and quiet fields. Up toward the Temple where the apex of the city lies and its incredible panorama. The city gives my gaze right back: shimmering and all aglow with promise. Percolating ideas now, rummaging in the memory for new connections. Winding paths continue to curl the feet to their way of thinking and together we walk across to the edge of the park. The land here has an aura, it seems to breathe with memories as you walk. Amongst some trees the various dishes and antennae of the telecommunications tower blossom from their reinforced concrete trunk. Through the perimeter, and the great expanse is left behind as side streets and semi-detached houses move into view, initially on one side then on both. Prestwich, accented north. Roundabout views onto the orbital motorway and looking west the difficult, personal tragedies of Death Valley beyond. Gazing back at the city, cars rushing in white or red noisy smears underneath, the sequestered towers hunkered into the landscape's bowl peek and blink in return. Another night beckons.

A manifesto for the nocturnal city

Cities are changing. Just as the transformations that occurred in much-documented major cities such as London, Paris and New York have been quickly reproduced the world over, so the nocturnal city is under significant threat. A full protest at these symptomatic shifts – and of course, more pointedly, at their causes – requires a collective. The collective reclamation of the urban night is important and perhaps more urgent than ever. However, it is not the concern of this book. Instead, I have sought to trace out different ways in which there is much to be discovered and enjoyed through direct experience of cities at night beyond practices of consumption. In order to do so I have necessarily drawn upon my own personal experiences of night-walking. In every sense this is flawed and limited, perhaps vitally so. To read this book as a blueprint for every conceivable encounter with the urban night would be to misunderstand its message. However, I hope that this, at times solipsistic, writing will be recognized for the overall framing it intends to gather. To go out into the night is a conclusive act. It heralds the end of the day and the beginning of a new time and place to explore. Not simply the urban landscape but also one's self: a chance to encounter and attend to our deepest sense of being. Ian Nairn regularly expounded his readers to go and see the various architectural highlights his predilections and incisive understanding of the built environment snagged along the way. By extension I would therefore urge the reader to explore the nocturnal city and 'go and be.'

We may well look back on this period of urban development and policy making as one of profound loss through the aggregation and unholy marriage of neo-liberal economics and rapacious venture manifest in buildings. Architecture certainly appears marginalized as a cultural and civic force but within the shadows there still remain the shards of promise and optimism. As is the case for so many things in a rapidly changing world – so it is for places and, of critical importance here, *times* – the signals for extinction appear to be gathering all around us. To lament what has been lost but never truly experienced is to reflect on an empty albeit burnished vessel. Far better to embrace the world and its contradictions, difficulties, untidiness and dirtiness, physical and psychic, than to summon long-vanished ghosts. From simply existing to meaningful becoming, the potential is out there for us all.

At the time of writing, the twenty-first century is still relatively nascent. Halfway through the second decade of the new millennium it seems evident that the harmful velocities of hyper-accelerated culture and commerce have profoundly affected how and who we are. Our capacity, if not necessarily our capability, to resist is compromised by the seemingly endless array of distractions that demand our responsiveness. Yet it is in this state of constant agitation that we appear productive. We feel we have accomplished something when we have responded to a number of emails, updated our status and location on social media. We have told everyone where we are, who we are with and how we are doing. The compulsion to partake in the collective amnesia of blurred identities and poor concentration is subtle but extremely seductive. Perhaps of equal importance, it has also significantly altered *when* we are. To this end, whatever the future of cities may hold, our relationship with them is likely to become further and further mediated and, thus, even more diluted. This is why attending to them is vital. Not as vapid arenas of consumption, but as the real deal, the twenty-first-century ecology of humanity. The rich and deep experiences that can be enjoyed in the city at night are out here, awaiting you. Unlike the rapidly disappearing qualities and objects of Nairn's London, the nocturnal city shifts in a different manner. Of course, some of the architecture may be razed and replaced, infrastructures upturned and updated, streets rerouted and rewired into the urban motherboard and memory of the city. But this is different. It is always in a state of becoming, never fully realized nor obliterated. The impossibility of standing in a stream in exactly the same place twice is akin to the urban night and its encounters. It is in flow; slowly melding and molten it shifts quietly. There is always difference, even when presented with uncanny simulacra of a previous jaunt.

Walking in cities at night, therefore, enables us to sense, connect and think with the city around us. We are able to give things our undivided attention, a welcome respite from the ongoing erosion and subdivision of our time and sense of belonging in the world. Deliberately moving out of the glare and stare of our commoditized and highly structured daily routines and into the rich shadows and patina of our cities at night may be one of the few truly beautiful and sublime practices available to us. Far from being dead hours, for the wakeful the night affords investigation and liberation. It is an essential part of living: an important counterpoint to responsibilities assumed in the daytime. The liquidity of the market has all but infiltrated every potential aspect of epicurean delight. We have become programmed within the call-and-response of contemporary culture to enjoy, if not actively seek, pleasures within the late-capitalist dome. Further, previously unimaginable dimensions of our lives have been effortlessly integrated into the market, not least our attention. I would therefore like to sketch out one alternative way of being. The variegated ways in which nightwalking enables moments in the construction of a truly new world to be understood is key to this framing. Slipping into the thick darkness of the nocturnal city is to leave inhibited preconceptions behind. The metricized daytime performance can remain, safely ensconced; be assured it will be awaiting your return. In the meantime the nighttime urban landscape offers a different realm: full of subtle resistances and challenges. We know it is easier to imagine the end of the world than the destruction of capitalism. The inertia that binds us within contemporary culture is discretely hidden behind multiple veils of the 'new' that, as discussed earlier, is anything but. However, we are also willing residents within such containment.

In the first half of the nineties, the British television adventure gameshow *The Crystal Maze* was aired. In each episode, a team was led through a series of puzzles and trials that had to be solved individually. Successful completion of these tasks culminated in extended access to the Crystal Dome, a Buckminster Fuller-derived geodesic glasshouse the scale of which was perhaps tellingly and disarmingly domestic. The objective for the team was to collect one-hundred gold foil tokens to win a prize. However, these were mixed with silver foil tokens, the number of which would be discounted from the total so in fact the team had to collect one-hundred more gold tokens than any silver ones collected. This predicament was given further drama by the turning on of wind machines beneath the dome, which ensured all the foil tokens were swept up in a beguiling swirl, fluttering around in an erratic fashion. Like the team of contestants in this final challenge we are cooperative and complicit in our collective frenzy to grab the shiny tokens amidst their fan-fuelled flurry in the air. Everything is exciting and tantalizing, all the more for being just slightly out of reach as we grasp. The real prize here is the constant state of distraction rather than the relative mediocrity of what is won. It is perhaps indicative of our ongoing preoccupation for apparent, gleaming newness amongst recycled ideas and movements that after twenty years, the game show has been developed as a live immersive experience for members of the public.

To suggest that we must abandon our daily roles and responsibilities or that the nocturnal city is an entirely different world within which we can explore would be misleading. Instead, rather than the liquidity of the daytime – easy-access, always-on, pervasive exploitation – the nighttime urban landscape offers what may be understood as *sublime liquidity*. By this term, I am referring to the awe-inspiring and complete nature of the urban night that exists as an offset overlay to the daytime city. In the study of chemistry, to be sublimed is defined as a process where a solid substance changes directly into vapour when heated, typically forming a solid deposit again on cooling. I believe this the state that the nocturnal city provides. The liquidity of the daytime can be bypassed, the palpable darkness and varying levels of light providing a rich landscape for exploration both physically and of the psyche. The nighttime city is full of opportunities to probe, examine and elucidate. It is deep canvas of merged grey-yellow-brown-orange-blacks that can always be added to. The personal inscriptions of nightwalking offer a place and time that need not sacrifice the other facets of your life, but enrich them. Through a thorough appreciation of thinking, sensing and connecting, walking at night can be a deep plunge into one's self. Ideologies, identities and creative expression can be forged and questioned here. The various costs borne by many people in order to attain modern lifestyles mean that relinquishing them in total is not a viable option. Nor need it be. One of the considerable pleasures of nightwalking is the personal character of it, to be engaged with at whatever frequency, duration and scale suitable to the individual. It opens up the city as well as our own selves. Walking with another person at night, both facing forward, gives shared outlook to the same experiences and an implicit confessional structure to the occurrence, which also may be highly beneficial. Walking alone, whilst perhaps unnerving to begin with, provides the full spectrum of intuition and multi-sensory attention to be navigated. Nightwalking promotes the city of the imagination to be constructed with each step, bringing forth a wealth of impressions and notions. It can be all-consuming or tentatively approached. To walk in the city at night is to extemporize. It is an opportunity to shed the creeping negative equity of the daytime and celebrate urban virtues, beauty in the ordinary. Released from the streamlined vectors of routine, richness beckons in nightwalking when the mysterious, the quiet, the secret and the itinerant may be explored in all their glory. It is an escape from the interdictions of daily life. It favours propinquity with the urban night. Rather than a time and place for the lurid or sharp vicissitudes of fortune, walking in the nocturnal city is an exaltation of endless discovery and joy in being alive, attuned and attentive to the immediate surroundings. In whichever of these ways appeals to you, or indeed any other route, before the sun rises again the sublime liquidity of the nocturnal city awaits you.

Go and be.

References

Amato, Joseph A. (2004). *On Foot: A History of Walking*. New York: New York University Press.

Aragon, Louis (1994). *Paris Peasant*. Translated and introduced by S. Watson Taylor. Boston, MA: Exact Change.

Attlee, James (2011). *Nocturne: A Journey in Search of Moonlight*. London: Hamish Hamilton.

Bakhtin, Mikhail Mikhailovich (1981). 'Forms of Time and of the Chronotope in the Novel.' *The Dialogic Imagination: Four Essays*. Edited by Michael Holquist. Translated by C. Emerson and M. Holquist. Austin, TX: University of Texas Press. pp. 84–258.

Baudrillard, Jean (1993). *The Transparency of Evil: Essays of Extreme Phenomena*. London: Verso.

Bauman, Zygmunt (2000). *Liquid Modernity*. Cambridge: Polity.

Beaumont, Matthew (2015). *Nightwalking: A Nocturnal History of London*. London: Verso.

Benjamin, Walter (2005). 'Moscow.' *Selected Writings*. Volume 2, part 1, 1927–1930. Edited by M.W. Jennings, H, Eiland and G. Smith. Cambridge, MA: The Belknap Press of Harvard University Press. pp. 22–46.

— (1978). 'A Berlin Chronicle.' *Reflections: Essays, Aphorisms, Autobiographical Writings*. New York: Harcourt Brace Jovanovich. pp. 3–60.

Bergson, Henri (2012). *The Creative Mind: An Introduction to Metaphysics*. New York: Dover Editions.

Berman, Marshall (1988). *All That Is Solid Melts Into Air: The Experience of Modernity*. London: Penguin.

Blomberg, Katja (2014). *Haus-Rucker-Co: Architekturutopie Reloaded*. Köln: Verlag der Buchhandlung Walther König.

Bogard, Paul (2013). *The End of Night: Searching for Natural Darkness in an Age of Artificial Light*. London: Fourth Estate.

Bressani, Martin (2015). 'Light into Darkness: Gaslight in Nineteenth Century Paris.' *Cities of Light: Two Centuries of Urban Illumination*. Edited by S. Isenstadt, M.M. Petty, and D. Neumann. Oxon: Routledge. pp. 28–36.

Burgin, Victor (1996). *Some Cities*. London: Reaktion.

Burke, Edmund (1757). 'A Philosophical Enquiry into the Origin of Our Ideas of the Sublime and Beautiful.' Available at: <http://www.gutenberg.org/files/15043/15043-h/15043-h.htm> [Accessed 12 September 2015].

Caillois, Roger (1987). 'Mimicry and Legendary Psychasthenia.' *October: The First Decade*. Translated by J. Shepley. Edited by A. Michelson, R. Krauss, D. Crimp and J. Copjec. Cambridge, MA: The MIT Press. pp. 58–74.

Calvino, Italo (1997). *Invisible Cities*. London: Vintage.

Careri, Francesco (2001). *Walkscapes: Walking as an Aesthetic Practice*. Barcelona: Gustavo Gili.

Castells, Manuel (2000). *The Rise of the Network Society*. 2nd Edition. London: Blackwell.

Corner, James (1999). 'Eidetic Operations and New Landscapes.' *Recovering Landscape: Essays in Contemporary Landscape Architecture*. New York: Princeton Architectural Press. pp. 153–169.

Crawford, Matthew B. (2015). *The World Beyond Your Head: On Becoming an Individual in an Age of Distraction*. London: Penguin.

Davis, Mike (1990). *City of Quartz: Excavating the Future in Los Angeles*. London: Verso.

De Muynck, Bert (2004). 'The Prosthetic Paradox.' *Angst & Ruimte / Fear & Space*. Rotterdam: NAi Publishers. pp. 8–15.

De Saint-Exupéry, Antoine (1986). *Flight to Arras*. Translated by L. Galantière. San Diego, CA: Harcourt, Inc.

Dun, Aidan A. (1995). *Vale Royal*. Uppingham: Goldmark.

Edensor, Tim (2013). 'Reconnecting with Darkness: Gloomy Landscapes, Lightless Places.' *Social & Cultural Geography*

14(4). pp. 446–65.

Ekirch, A. Roger (2005). *At Day's Close: A History of Nighttime.* London: Weidenfeld & Nicolson.

Farley, Paul and Michael Symmons Roberts (2011). *Edgelands: Journeys into England's True Wilderness.* London: Jonathan Cape.

Fisher, Mark (2009). *Capitalist Realism: Is There No Alternative?* Winchester: Zero Books.

Gatt, Caroline (2013). 'Vectors, direction of attention and unprotected backs: Re-specifying relations in anthropology.' *Anthropological Theory*, 13(4). pp. 347–369.

Gibson, James Jerome (1979). *The Ecological Approach to Visual Perception.* Hillsdale, NJ: Lawrence Erlbaum Associates.

Glaeser, Edward (2011). *Triumph of the City: How our greatest Invention Makes Us Richer, Smarter, Greener, Healthier, and Happier.* London: Penguin.

Gros, Frédéric (2014). *A Philosophy of Walking.* London: Verso.

Harris, Michael (2014). *The End of Absence: Reclaiming What We've Lost in a World of Constant Connection.* London: Penguin.

Herron, Jerry (2010). 'Borderland/Borderama/Detroit.' *Distributed Urbanism: Cities After Google Earth.* Edited by Gretchen Wilkins. London: Routledge. pp. 63–86.

Hollis, Leo (2013). *Cities Are Good for You: The Genius of the Metropolis.* London: Bloomsbury.

Ingold, Tim (2011). *Being Alive: Essays on Movement, Knowledge and Decscription.* London: Routledge.

Jacobs, Jane (1961). *The Death and Life of Great American Cities.* New York: Random House.

Jacobs, Steven (2002). 'Shreds of Boring Postcards: Towards a Posturban Aesthetics of the Generic and the Everyday.' *Post Ex Sub Dis: Urban Fragmentations and Constructions.* Edited by Ghent Urban Studies Team. Rotterdam: 010 Publishers. pp. 15–64.

Jefferies, Richard (2012). *Nature Near London.* London: Collins.

Keiller, Patrick (2013). *The View from the Train: Cities and Other Landscapes*. London: Verso.

Kolsofsky, Craig (2011). *Evening's Empire: A History of Night in Early Modern Europe*. Cambridge: Cambridge University Press.

Kwinter, Sanford (2010). *Requiem: For The City At The End Of The Millennium*. Barcelona: Actar.

Lefebvre, Henri (1991). *The Production of Space*. Translated by D. Nicholson-Smith. Oxford: Blackwell.

Lévesque, Luc (2002). 'The "Terrain Vague" as Material – Some Observations.' Available at: < http://www.amarrages.com/textes_terrain.html> [Accessed 17 September 2015].

Lynch, Kevin (1960). *The Image of the City*. Cambridge, MA: The MIT Press.

— (1972). *What Time Is This Place?* Cambridge, MA: The MIT Press.

Mabey, Richard (2010). *The Unofficial Countryside*. Dorset: Little Toller Books.

Macfarlane, Robert (2015). *Landmarks*. London: Hamish Hamilton.

Machen, Arthur (1924). *The London Adventure, or The Art of Wandering*. London: Martin Secker.

Manaugh, Geoff (2013). *Landscape Futures: Instruments, Devices and Architectural Inventions*. Barcelona: Actar.

Melbin, Murray (1987). *Night as Frontier: colonizing the world after dark*. New York: The Free Press/Macmillan.

Miéville, China (2009). *The City & The City*. London: Macmillan.

Minkowski, E. 1933. 'Le temps vécu.' *Etudes phénoménologiques et psychopathologiques*. Paris. pp. 382–398.

Minton, Anna (2009). *Ground Control: Fear and happiness in the twenty-first-century city*. London: Penguin.

Montgomery, Charles (2013). *Happy City: Transforming our lives through urban design*. London: Penguin.

Muir, John (1979). *John of the Mountains: The Unpublished Journals of John Muir*. Edited by L.M. Wolfe. Madison, WI: University of

Wisconsin Press.

Mumford, Lewis (1938). *The Culture of Cities*. New York: Harcourt, Brace.

Nairn, Ian (1966). *Nairn's London*. London: Penguin.

Nicholson, Geoff (1997). *Bleeding London*. London: Victor Gollancz.

Offenhuber, Dietmar and Carlo Ratti (2014). *Decoding the City: How Big Data Can Change Urbanism*. Berlin: Birkhäuser.

Pallasmaa, Juhani (2005). *The Eyes of the Skin: Architecture and the Senses*. New York: John Wiley.

Palmer, Bryan D. (2000). *Cultures of Darkness: Night Travels in the Histories of Transgression*. New York: Monthly Review Press.

Papadimitriou, Nick (2012). *Scarp: In Search of London's Outer Limits*. London: Sceptre.

Raban, Jonathan (1974). *Soft City*. London: Hamish Hamilton.

Sandhu, Sukhdev (2007). *Night Haunts: A journey through the London night*. London: Artangel and Verso.

Schivelbusch, Wolfgang (1995). *Disenchanted Night: The Industrialization of Light in the Nineteenth Century*. Berkeley and Los Angeles, CA: University of California Press.

Schlör, Joachim (2013). *Nights in the Big City*. Translated by P.G. Imhof and D.R. Roberts. London: Reaktion.

Sennett, Richard (1994). *Flesh and Stone: The Body and the City in Western Civilization*. London: Faber.

Simmel, Georg (1997). 'The sociology of space.' In D. Frisby and M. Featherstone (eds). *Simmel on Culture*. London, Sage. pp. 137–185.

Sinclair, Iain (1997). *Lights Out for the Territory*. London: Granta Books.

Solnit, Rebecca (2000). *Wanderlust: A History of Walking*. London: Penguin.

Southwood, Ivor (2011). *Non-Stop Inertia*. Winchester: Zero Books.

Talanova, Julia (2015). '9/11 tribute lights briefly shut off after birds get trapped.' *CNN*. Available at: <http://edition. cnn.com/2015/09/12/us/9-11-tribute-lights-off/> [Accessed 14 September 2015].

UNFPA (2007). *State Of The World Population 2007: Unleashing the Potential of Urban Growth.* UNFPA: New York.

Vidler, Anthony (1992). 'Dark Space.' *The Architectural Uncanny.* Cambridge, MA: The MIT Press. pp. 167–175.

Virilio, Paul (2000). The Big Night. *A Landscape of Events.* Translated by J. Rose. Cambridge, MA: The MIT Press. pp. 2–11.

Williams, Heathcote (1991). *Autogeddon.* London: Jonathan Cape.

Williams, Robert (2008). 'Night Spaces: Darkness, Deterritorialization, and Social Control.' *Space and Culture,* November; vol. 11 (4). pp. 514–532.

Zumthor, Peter (2006). *Atmospheres: Architectural Environments – Surrounding Objects.* Berlin: Birkhäuser.

Contemporary culture has eliminated both the concept of the
public and the figure of the intellectual. Former public spaces –
both physical and cultural – are now either derelict or colonized
by advertising. A cretinous anti-intellectualism presides,
cheerled by expensively educated hacks in the pay of
multinational corporations who reassure their bored readers
that there is no need to rouse themselves from their interpassive
stupor. The informal censorship internalized and propagated by
the cultural workers of late capitalism generates a banal
conformity that the propaganda chiefs of Stalinism could only
ever have dreamt of imposing. Zer0 Books knows that another
kind of discourse – intellectual without being academic, popular
without being populist – is not only possible: it is already
flourishing, in the regions beyond the striplit malls of so-called
mass media and the neurotically bureaucratic halls of the
academy. Zer0 is committed to the idea of publishing as a
making public of the intellectual. It is convinced that in
the unthinking, blandly consensual culture in which we live,
critical and engaged theoretical reflection is more important
than ever before.

ZERO BOOKS

Capitalist Realism Is there no alternative?
Mark Fisher
An analysis of the ways in which capitalism has presented itself as the only realistic political-economic system.
Paperback: November 27, 2009 978-1-84694-317-1 $14.95 £7.99.
ebook: July 1, 2012 978-1-78099-734-6 $9.99 £6.99.

The Wandering Who? A study of Jewish identity politics
Gilad Atzmon
An explosive unique crucial book tackling the issues of Jewish Identity Politics and ideology and their global influence.
Paperback: September 30, 2011 978-1-84694-875-6 $14.95 £8.99.
ebook: September 30, 2011 978-1-84694-876-3 $9.99 £6.99.

Clampdown Pop-cultural wars on class and gender
Rhian E. Jones
Class and gender in Britpop and after, and why 'chav' is a feminist issue.
Paperback: March 29, 2013 978-1-78099-708-7 $14.95 £9.99.
ebook: March 29, 2013 978-1-78099-707-0 $7.99 £4.99.

The Quadruple Object
Graham Harman
Uses a pack of playing cards to present Harman's metaphysical system of fourfold objects, including human access, Heidegger's indirect causation, panpsychism and ontography.
Paperback: July 29, 2011 978-1-84694-700-1 $16.95 £9.99.

Weird Realism Lovecraft and Philosophy
Graham Harman
As Hölderlin was to Martin Heidegger and Mallarmé to Jacques Derrida, so is H.P. Lovecraft to the Speculative Realist philosophers.
Paperback: September 28, 2012 978-1-78099-252-5 $24.95 £14.99.
ebook: September 28, 2012 978-1-78099-907-4 $9.99 £6.99.

Sweetening the Pill or How We Got Hooked on Hormonal Birth Control
Holly Grigg-Spall
Is it really true? Has contraception liberated or oppressed women?
Paperback: September 27, 2013 978-1-78099-607-3 $22.95 £12.99.
ebook: September 27, 2013 978-1-78099-608-0 $9.99 £6.99.

Why Are We The Good Guys? Reclaiming Your Mind From The Delusions Of Propaganda
David Cromwell
A provocative challenge to the standard ideology that Western power is a benevolent force in the world.
Paperback: September 28, 2012 978-1-78099-365-2 $26.95 £15.99.
ebook: September 28, 2012 978-1-78099-366-9 $9.99 £6.99.

The Truth about Art Reclaiming quality
Patrick Doorly
The book traces the multiple meanings of art to their various sources, and equips the reader to choose between them.
Paperback: August 30, 2013 978-1-78099-841-1 $32.95 £19.99.

Bells and Whistles More Speculative Realism
Graham Harman
In this diverse collection of sixteen essays, lectures, and interviews Graham Harman lucidly explains the principles of Speculative Realism, including his own object-oriented philosophy.

Paperback: November 29, 2013 978-1-78279-038-9 $26.95 £15.99.
ebook: November 29, 2013 978-1-78279-037-2 $9.99 £6.99.

Towards Speculative Realism: Essays and Lectures Essays and Lectures
Graham Harman
These writings chart Harman's rise from Chicago sportswriter to co founder of one of Europe's most promising philosophical movements: Speculative Realism.
Paperback: November 26, 2010 978-1-84694-394-2 $16.95 £9.99.
ebook: January 1, 1970 978-1-84694-603-5 $9.99 £6.99.

Meat Market Female flesh under capitalism
Laurie Penny
A feminist dissection of women's bodies as the fleshy fulcrum of capitalist cannibalism, whereby women are both consumers and consumed.
Paperback: April 29, 2011 978-1-84694-521-2 $12.95 £6.99.
ebook: May 21, 2012 978-1-84694-782-7 $9.99 £6.99.

Translating Anarchy The Anarchism of Occupy Wall Street
Mark Bray
An insider's account of the anarchists who ignited Occupy Wall Street.
Paperback: September 27, 2013 978-1-78279-126-3 $26.95 £15.99.
ebook: September 27, 2013 978-1-78279-125-6 $6.99 £4.99.

One Dimensional Woman
Nina Power
Exposes the dark heart of contemporary cultural life by examining pornography, consumer capitalism and the ideology of women's work.
Paperback: November 27, 2009 978-1-84694-241-9 $14.95 £7.99.
ebook: July 1, 2012 978-1-78099-737-7 $9.99 £6.99.

Dead Man Working
Carl Cederstrom, Peter Fleming
An analysis of the dead man working and the way in which
capital is now colonizing life itself.
Paperback: May 25, 2012 978-1-78099-156-6 $14.95 £9.99.
ebook: June 27, 2012 978-1-78099-157-3 $9.99 £6.99.

Unpatriotic History of the Second World War
James Heartfield
The Second World War was not the Good War of legend. James
Heartfield explains that both Allies and Axis powers fought for
the same goals - territory, markets and natural resources.
Paperback: September 28, 2012 978-1-78099-378-2 $42.95 £23.99.
ebook: September 28, 2012 978-1-78099-379-9 $9.99 £6.99.

Find more titles at www.zero-books.net